A Doubleday *IMAG*

SAINTS FOR SINNERS

ALBAN GOODIER, S.J.

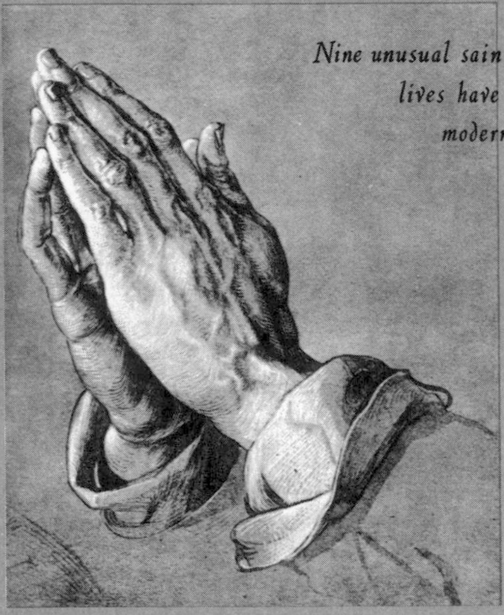

Nine unusual saints whose inspiring lives have significance for modern men and women

Complete and Unabridged

IMAGE D88

In SAINTS FOR SINNERS, Archbishop Goodier, in extremely readable and inspiring style, has brought the lives of nine unusual saints into remarkably clear focus. Skillfully depicting each underlying personality, he has perceptively and dramatically portrayed the individual's iniquitous existence, eventual capitulation to God's grace, and ensuing ascent to sanctity.

As the life of each saint is developed, it becomes forcefully evident to the reader how each one yielded to sins and imperfections common to all of us: lust, aridity, despondence, mediocrity, aimlessness, or despair. Yet each of them, fettered by faults, ultimately and courageously emerged from depths of degradation and achieved sublime heights of piety and spirituality.

All nine biographies graphically emphasize the constant and arduous battle against evil, whether it be in the fifth century of Augustine, the sixteenth century of Francis Xavier or the twentieth century in which we are struggling today. One factor is strikingly apparent: each saint included in SAINTS FOR SINNERS was an ordinary human being, subject to ordinary human deficiencies. The vicissitudes, temptations, and shortcomings they conquered are startlingly comparable to those faced by modern men and women. Because of the uphill fight each of these saints waged and won, it becomes obvious that no obstacle to sanctity is insurmountable.

Archbishop Goodier's most important point is that there is a latent potentiality in each sinner to become a saint. Since all of us are sinners, SAINTS FOR SINNERS is encouraging proof that there is in each of us the substance for sainthood.

ALBAN GOODIER, S.J.

❦❖❦ SAINTS ❦❖❦
FOR SINNERS

❦❖❦

IMAGE BOOKS

A DIVISION OF DOUBLEDAY & COMPANY, INC.
GARDEN CITY, NEW YORK

IMAGE BOOKS EDITION 1959

by special arrangement with Sheed & Ward, Inc.

Image Books edition published September, 1959
1st printing .... August, 1959
2nd printing .... November, 1960

Printed in the United States of America

COVER BY EILEEN TABER
TYPOGRAPHY BY JOSEPH P. ASCHERL

THE FOOLISH THINGS OF THE WORLD
HATH GOD CHOSEN
THAT HE MAY CONFOUND THE WISE
AND THE WEAK THINGS OF THE WORLD
HATH GOD CHOSEN
THAT HE MAY CONFOUND THE STRONG
AND THE BASE THINGS OF THE WORLD
AND THE THINGS THAT ARE CONTEMPTIBLE
HATH GOD CHOSEN
AND THINGS THAT ARE NOT
THAT HE MIGHT BRING TO NOUGHT THINGS THAT ARE
THAT NO FLESH SHOULD GLORY IN HIS SIGHT.

I Corinthians 1:27–29

CONTENTS

PREFACE

Is this a book of biography, or is it romance? The author himself scarcely knows. If an honest attempt to give the facts makes biography, then he hopes it may deserve that title. If an effort to interpret some of those facts and give them life makes romance, then must his work be called romantic. In either case he hopes that the picture in each case is true; and that the whole is a proof of a deeper truth which it is needful for us all to remember. It is, that "God is wonderful in His saints"; that He "chooses whom He will Himself"; that in His house "there are many mansions"; and that there is no condition of life to which His grace does not reach, none so low but He can make it worthy of Himself.

We have called this book "Saints for Sinners," and in doing so we would take the word "Sinners" in a broad sense. For beside the actual consciousness of sin, and the sense of weakness that comes of it, there is also a kindred consciousness of failure, and ineffectualness, and other hard things in the spiritual life which makes us realise our utter nothingness, and compels us sometimes to wonder whether we are not ourselves their cause. When these hard things oppress us, and tempt us to despair or resent, it is well to bear in mind that they were the lot of all the saints, that "virtue is made perfect in infirmity," and that the life of the Cross is an ideal above every other, however human nature may stumble or be scandalised. For this reason, in these chapters, the human element has been more considered than the sanctity that has been built upon it; the latter rises in proportion to the depth of the foundation.

For permission to include in this book three studies, with some additions, which have already appeared in the *Month*, the author is deeply grateful to its Editor.

SAINTS FOR SINNERS

ST. AUGUSTINE OF HIPPO

354–430

Men approach St. Augustine with mixed feelings. So high does he tower above those of his generation, perhaps above those of every generation, that they look up to him with a certain awe, almost with fear. The very sight of his works, more, probably, than those of any other writer of the past, frightens us and puts us off; someone has seriously said that merely to read what Augustine has written would take an ordinary man a life-time. Nevertheless, to one who will have courage and come near, it is strange how human, and even how little in his greatness, Augustine is found to be. "I liked to play": *delectabat ludere,* he said of himself in his childhood; and there is something of that same delight to be found in him to the very end of his days.

Augustine was born in Thagaste, a Roman town in Numidia, North Africa. It was a free town, and also a market-town, set at a place where many Roman roads converged; to it the caravans from east and west brought their merchandise, in it the luxury of Rome was repeated, with the added freedom of Africa. He was the eldest son of one Patricius, a well-to-do citizen of the place, a pagan but not a fanatic, whose ideal of life was to get the most out of it he could, without being too particular as to the means. Patricius, at the age of forty, had married Monica, a girl of seventeen, a Christian on both her father's and her mother's side. This marriage alone would seem to imply a certain laxity of faith in the family; the fact that Monica owed most of her religious and moral training to an old nurse confirms it.

It cannot be said that the marriage was a happy one. Perhaps it was not intended to be; it was a marriage of convenience and no more. For the pagan Patricius it meant life with a woman who, the older she became, and the more difficult her situation, clung the more to her own religion, and would have nothing to do with his free and easy ways, to call them by no worse name. For Monica it meant a life of constant self-suppression; of abuse even to blows, for Patricius had fits of violent temper; of slander on the part of those who were only too anxious to pander to Patricius, or were jealous of the influence her meek disposition had upon him. Three children were born to them, Augustine the first, but none of them were baptized. In those days a middle course was found. As children were born they were inscribed as catechumens; the baptism might come later, perhaps whenever there was danger of death.

Augustine grew up among pagan children, apparently in a pagan school, and his morals from the first were no better than theirs. He could steal, he could cheat, he could lie with the best of them; to do these things cleverly and successfully was a mark of talent rather than of vice. He went to school, and he hated it, both its restraint, and the things he had to learn. He was thrashed repeatedly, and when he came home received little commiseration, even from his own mother. His boyhood, from his own description, was an unhappy time; it tended to make him all the more bitter and reckless. But he was a precociously clever child, and in spite of his thrashings, which only made him more obstinate, and his own idleness, he learned more than his companions. Both his father and his mother became ambitious for him; they decided to give him a better education than could be given him in Thagaste. He was sent to Madaura, a prosperous city thirty miles away.

But thirty miles, in those days, and for a boy such as

Augustine, was a great, separating distance. Here at last he was his own master; the longing he had always had to do just what he liked, without let or hindrance from anyone, was allowed free scope. He studied the pagan classics, for he loved to read and read; he studied not only their literature, but also their ideals and their life. These were exemplified all around him, and he could take part in them as much as he pleased; the pursuit of pleasure at all costs, the wild orgies of the carnivals of Bacchus, the worship of the decadent Roman ideal, smart, sensual, excusing, boldly daring, laughing with approval at every excess of sinful love. Such was the atmosphere the clever, imaginative, craving, reckless Augustine was made to breathe in the city of Apuleius at the age of fifteen; and to face it he had nothing but the flattering encouragement of a pagan father, the timid fear of a Christian mother whose religion he had already learned to despise. He soon became simply a pagan, a non-moral pagan at the most critical time of his life.

The consequences were inevitable. Augustine came home from Madaura addicted to the lowest vices. What was worse, he seemed to have no conscience left; worse still, he had a father who looked upon the same excess as a proof of manhood, the sowing of wild oats now which gave promise of great things later. Only one chain held him, the love he had for his mother. He laughed at her pious ways, he deliberately defied and hurt her; but underneath, though he tried not to own it to himself, his respect and admiration and affection for her had steadily increased. It was the same on her side, which made the bond all the stronger. Monica's life with her husband had been unhappy and loveless; and the love she longed to give was poured out on her favourite yet reckless son. The more she loved him, the more she was appalled at the life he was already living, and at the future to which it must inevitably lead. She blamed herself for having been partially the cause of his downfall. She had encouraged the plan of his going to Madaura; she had given him little to protect him while he was there; she would do all she could to win him back, though it was to be the struggle of a life-time. This made her strive all the more for her own perfection; if she was to influence him at all she must herself be true. Since she could say little to him, she would pray for him; she watched him, but it could only be from a distance. And Augustine, though he made nothing of it at the time, though he often took delight in hurting her by his boast of wickedness, knew nevertheless that she prayed, and watched, and loved; and he returned that love, and it grew.

The next step in Augustine's career was to Carthage. It was the centre of learning and pleasure in North Africa, and Augustine craved for both. There he lived, from the age of seventeen, learning and loving as he wished, for there was no one to check or guide him. "I went to Carthage," he wrote later, "where shameful love bubbled round me like boiling oil." But he was wise enough to know that this was the opportunity of his life; in the midst of his evil living he worked hard. At this point his father died, a Christian at the last, which cannot but have had an effect on the son; and the pinch of poverty, in consequence of the death, made him work all the harder. He soon became known as the gayest, the most gifted, the most sensual scholar in the University of Carthage; a three-fold triumph, of each of which he was proud. In the schools of Rhetoric his declamations were proposed to other students as models; outside the schools he was admired and courted as the reckless votary of love.

But the ways of God are strange. One day, in the midst of this thoughtless life, he was studying Cicero. He lighted on the following passage:

"If man has a soul, as the greatest philosophers maintain, and if that soul is immortal and divine, then must it needs be that the more it has been steeped in reason, and true love, and the pursuit of truth, and the less it has been stained by vice and passion, so much the more surely it will rise above this earth and ascend into the skies."

This sentence, suddenly come upon, was, he tells us, the beginning of light. It made him restless; his eyes continually went back to it; he began to ask himself whether, after all, he was as happy as he affected. He looked for a solution elsewhere, whether a confirmation of the teaching, or a quieting of his conscience, he did not care. He paid more attention to the other pagan philosophers, but they did not lead him far. He took to the Bible, and for a time it held him; but soon that, too, became insipid, and he put it away. He knew something about the Manichees, with their doctrine of a good and an evil spirit. They claimed to have a solution for all such problems; above all they pretended to solve them without too much surrender of the good things of this world. Sin could not be resisted, passion was a necessity; the doctrine suited Augustine very well as a check to this new thing, conscience, and he accepted it. Augustine became a Manichee.

We may now leap over some years. Augustine returned to Thagaste, and there set up a school; his restless soul soon tired of it, the provincialism of the place stifled him, and he went once more to Carthage. There he opened another school of Rhetoric; it was a great success, but being a youth of little over twenty he had need to supplement his knowledge with further reading. Nothing came amiss to this voracious mind; he read anything and everything that came in his way, the classics, the occult sciences, astrology, the fine arts. Meanwhile, more as a practice in dialectic than from any sense of conviction, he set himself to the task of converting his friends to Manicheism, and in part succeeded. At last, again grown restless, and devoured with an ambition for which Carthage had grown too small, he decided to seek his fortune in Rome, the centre and capital of the whole world. In spite of his mother's appeals, in spite of remonstrance from the woman he had ruined but who had been faithful to him, he eluded them both and slipped away, to make a name for himself as a conjuror in words in the heart of the Empire.

But the design of God was very different. Augustine's

sojourn in Rome was anything but the success he had anticipated. Scarcely had he arrived when he fell ill, and had to depend on the charity of condescending friends till he recovered, a fact which galled him exceedingly. As soon as he was well, he set about drawing pupils round him; this, in self-occupied, bustling Rome, was a more difficult matter than it had been in Carthage or Thagaste. Moreover the climate and the life of the place began to tell upon him. He could not endure its stifling air, its cobbled and uneven streets, while the coarseness of its manners disgusted this man of the world who, though steeped in vice as much as any Roman, still insisted on refinement. The gluttony and drunkenness he saw everywhere about him, the coarse outcries raised from time to time, in the theatres and elsewhere, against all foreign immigrants, the lack of interest in things intellectual even among those who claimed to be most cultured, the childish imitation, among the rich and so-called upper classes, of eastern splendour and extravagance, the multitudinous temples of all kinds of gods, disgorging every day their besotted votaries—the heart of Rome being eaten out by the serpent of Asia—the contempt for human life, above all for the life of a slave or a captured foe, all these things, in spite of his own depravity, began to tell upon his mind. He was more alone now, and was forced to reflect; his life was in the making and he had to look into the future; if he continued to sin, to his own disgust he found that he did so, not because it satisfied any desire, or because it gave him any pleasure, but because he could not help it. He knew that he was its slave, whatever he might appear, however he might boast of liberty. Long since had Manicheism lost its hold upon him; as he had once used his dialectic in its favour, so now it amused him to tear it to tatters. He clung to it still, for it provided him with a convenient cloak with which to cover and excuse the life which he was at present powerless to check; but in his heart he did not believe in its tenets any longer.

Then another force came into his life. Augustine had

kept his school open in Rome with no little difficulty, not because he was not successful, but because his pupils would often go away leaving him unpaid. From sheer and undeserved poverty, it seemed he would have to return to Africa. Suddenly a professor's chair at Milan was offered for competition, and Milan, for many reasons, had come to mean more to Augustine than Rome itself. Milan, not Rome, was now the city of the Emperor and his court; Milan was the centre of culture and fashion; above all, it was the home of Ambrose, and Ambrose was a name that was ever on the lips of any master of rhetoric. Augustine competed for the post, and with the help of sundry friends obtained it. He went to Milan; he sought out Ambrose, first to criticise and judge as a master of letters, later to discover a friend. It was not long before, to his own surprise, he was pouring out his now miserable soul into the bishop's ear.

Still that did not come all at once. It would seem that the plain straightforward Roman, though a better scholar, in many ways, than Augustine, never quite understood the eager, melancholy, sensitive and sensuous African, who, nevertheless, was by this time straining for a guide to lead him to the truth. The days passed on into years. The young and ambitious rhetorician had found solid ground at last, and Milan took him to its heart. Great men and wealthy noticed him, invited him to their mansions; Augustine began to tell himself that he could wish for nothing better than to be as one of them. He would settle down, content with that goal; he would marry and become respectable, according to the standard of these men of the world; he would put away the woman he had wronged, and the rest would easily be condoned. He made a first step—and he failed; the ending of one fascination did but open the way to another. He told himself that he could not help but sin; it was part of his nature, his manner of life had made it a necessity. Then why trouble any more? One day, as he came home from a triumphant speech delivered before the Emperor, drunk with the praises showered on him, an intoxicated man lurched across his path, revelling in coarse merriment. Why should he not live as that man lived? Not, it was true, in the same brutish way; but there was a drunkenness that would suit him, which would let him live for the day, without giving the rest a moment's reflexion.

Nevertheless, as all this self-questioning showed, a new thing had awakened in him, and he could not make it sleep. He listened to Ambrose when he preached, ostensibly to study him as a rhetorician; he came away forgetting the rhetoric, but with a burning arrow in his heart. More and more he saw what he must do, if he would be even what his own ideal of himself pictured to him; he saw it, but to do it was quite another thing. He listened to the Church's liturgy; he watched the people at their prayers in full contentment all around him; he longed even to tears that he might be one with them. Still he could not bring himself to pay the price. Let us listen to him here as he tells the story of his conflict at this time. Thus he writes:

"O my God, let me with a thankful heart remember and confess to thee thy mercies on me. Let my very bones be steeped in thy love, and let them cry out: Who is like to thee, O Lord? (Ps. 35, 10) Thou hast broken my bonds asunder; I will offer to thee the sacrifice of thanksgiving (Ps. 116, 16, 17). How thou hast broken them openly I will declare; and all who adore thee, when they hear my tale, shall say: Blessed is the Lord, in heaven and on earth; great and glorious is His name.

"The enemy held my will captive; therefore he kept me, chained down and bound. For out of a froward will lust had sprung; and lust pampered had become custom; and custom indulged had become necessity. These were the links of the chain; this was the bondage in which I was bound, and that new will which was already born in me, freely to serve thee, wholly to enjoy thee, O God, the only true joy, was not yet able to subdue my former wilfulness, strengthened by the wantonness of years. So did my two wills, one new, the other old, one spiritual, the other carnal, fight within me, and by their discord undo my soul."

More and more the truth grew upon him, yet Augustine could not bring himself to act. In a succession of passages he dwells upon his hesitation; they are among the most tragically dramatic pages that he ever wrote. Let us hear some of them.

"Thou didst on all sides shew me that what thou didst say was true, and by the truth I was convicted. I had nothing at all to answer but those dull and dreary words: Anon, anon; or, Presently; or, Leave me alone but a little while. But my Presently, presently, came to no present, and my Little while lasted long."

"What words did I not use against myself! With scourges of condemnation I lashed my soul, to force it to follow me in my effort to go after thee. Yet it drew back; it refused to follow, and without a word of excuse. Its arguments were confuted, its self-defence was spent. There remained no more than mute shrinking; it feared, as it would death itself, to have that disease of habit healed whereby it was wasting to death."

"Thus I lay, soul-sick and tormented, chiding myself more vehemently than ever, rolling and writhing in my bondage, longing for the fetter to be wholly broken which alone now held me, but yet did hold me secure. And thou, O Lord, didst harry me within with thy merciless mercy; thou didst multiply the lashes of fear and shame, lest I should again give way, and lest I should fail to break this last remaining bond, and it should recover strength, and bind me down the faster. I said within myself: Let it be done at once, let it be done now; and even as I spoke I all but did it. I all but did it, but I did it not. Still I sank back to my former place; I stood where I was and took breath again. Once more I tried, and wanted somewhat less to make me succeed, and again somewhat less, and I all but touched and laid hold of the object of my longing; yet again

I came not at it, nor touched it, nor laid hold of it. I still recoiled; I would not die to death that I might live to life."

"These petty toys of toys, these vanities of vanities, my longtime fascinations, still held me. They plucked at the garment of my flesh, and murmured caressingly: Dost thou cast us off? From this moment are we to be with thee no more for ever? From this moment shall this delight or that be no more lawful for thee for ever?"

"The time came when I scarcely heard them. For now they did not openly appear, they did not contradict me; instead they stood as it were behind my back, and muttered their lament, and pulled furtively at my cloak, and begged me, as I stood to go, but to look back on them once more. Thus did their shackles hinder me, and I shrank from shaking myself free from them, that I might burst my bonds and leap forward whither I was called. At the last some habit would whisper in my ear: Dost thou think that thou canst live without these things?"

But the liberation came at last. Monica, his mother, had prayed on; she had long since come to Milan to be near her son. She had shared his successes with him, and had even joined in the congratulations; but most of her time had been spent in the church, so much so that she had won the attention of Ambrose the Bishop. One day, on meeting Augustine, he congratulated him on having such a mother. That chance word, it would seem, was the beginning of the last act in the drama. Augustine was flattered with a worthy flattering; he was glad for his mother's sake and his own, and the love within began to take on a new warmth. On such little things may great destinies depend. And in the meantime, Augustine himself, though continually beaten, did not give up the struggle. If he could not face the hardest ordeal, at least he could do something. One by one he pushed the shackles away; first the bondage that compelled him to live in sin, then that of his false philosophy. Next he ceased to be even by profession a Manichee. Last of all he laid aside his office as municipal orator; it is a proof of the refining process through which he had by this time gone when he tells us that he had grown ashamed of the lies he had to tell for the sake of beautiful language.

At length the final grace came, and Augustine received it. "I was tired of devouring time and of being devoured by it," he writes; he must decide one way or the other. He had come to Milan a sceptic; he had by this time left that far behind. The evidence of a loving and a patient God, the truth of Jesus Christ, the peace and contentment of those who received Him and lived by Him, the summing up of all the philosophers had to say in the teaching of the Bible, the example of great men before him, who had suffered as he now suffered, had seen as he was now beginning to see, had made the leap and had found rest and peace, all these things crowded in upon him, and he knew what he should do. On the other hand was the surrender, the tearing away from all those things, good and evil, which hitherto had made life sweet, or at least as sweet as one like him could ever hope to find it. He could not do it. He despised himself for his hesitation but he could not move. He despised the Roman world which he now knew so well but he could not leave it. Besides, by this time he was ill; he was not himself. To make a change under these conditions was imprudent; when he was well again, he would never be able to persevere, and to fall back, once he had repented, would be only to make his second state worse than the first. He could not decide; even if he decided, it seemed to him that he could not make himself act. He must get someone to help him. He could not go to Ambrose; Ambrose had done for him all he was able and yet so far had failed. There was an old man, Simplicianus; he had been the confessor of Ambrose. In desperation he would go to him.

And Simplicianus received him, and humoured him; humoured him even in his pride, pointing out to him the nobility of truth and sacrifice. There were set before Augustine pictures of St. Antony in the desert and his followers, the hermits of Egypt, who at that time were the talk of Christian Rome. They had surrendered all; yet they were simple men with not much learning. Augustine was in his garden; he thought he was alone. He lay down beneath a tree; his tears wet the ground.

"How long?" he cried, "how long shall this be? It is always to-morrow and to-morrow. Why not this hour an end to all my meanness?"

As he spoke a little child in a house close by was singing some kind of nursery-rhyme, and the refrain was this: "Take up and read, take up and read." Mechanically Augustine stretched out his hand to a book he had brought with him. It was St. Paul's Epistles. He took it up, opened it at random, and read:

"Put ye on the Lord Jesus Christ, and make not provision for the flesh to fulfil the lusts thereof."

Suddenly all was quiet. He knew his decision had been made, and that he had the power to execute it. There was no more trouble, Augustine rose from where he lay, went into his mother's room, and there at her feet surrendered his past for ever. Soon he was at the feet of Ambrose; he had been lost and now at last he had found himself. He was at the time just thirty-three years of age. He celebrates his victory in the following passage:

"O Lord, I am thy servant; I am thy servant and the son of thy handmaid. Thou hast broken my bonds asunder; I will offer to thee the sacrifice of praise (Ps. 116, 16, 17). Let my heart and my tongue praise thee; yea, let all my bones say: O Lord, who is like to thee? Let them proclaim it; and do thou in return answer me, and say unto my soul: I am thy salvation (Ps. 35, 10). Who am I, and what am I? What an evil thing have been my deeds, or if not my deeds my words, or if not my words my will? But thou, O Lord, art good and merciful, and thy right hand hath reached down into the abysmal blackness of my death, and from the bottom of my heart hath emptied out its deep of

corruption. And thy gift was this, no longer to will what I
willed, but to will what thou didst will. How came it that
after all those years, after it was lost in that deep and dark-
some labyrinth, my free will was called forth in a moment
to submit my neck to thy easy yoke, and my shoulders to
thy light burthen, O Christ Jesus, my Helper and my Re-
deemer (Ps. 19, 4)? How sweet did it at once become to
me to be without the sweetness of those baubles! What I
feared to be parted from, it was now a joy to part with.
For thou didst cast them from me, thou the true and richest sweetness. Thou didst cast them forth, and in their
place didst substitute thyself, sweeter than all delight,
though not to flesh and blood, brighter than all light, but
more hidden than the lowest deep, higher than all honour,
but not to them that are high in their own conceits. Now
my soul was free; . . . and my infant tongue spoke to thee
freely, my light, my riches, my health, the Lord my God."

For the purposes of this study we do not need to follow
Augustine too closely through the rest of his career. He was
still, to the world about him, the brilliant professor of
Milan; only a few of his friends knew of the change that
had taken place. He would continue his lectures; there
should be no sensation about him. But his health, never
strong, had been shaken by the ordeal; it gave him a reason
to retire to the villa of a friend at Cassicium, and there for
a time he took up his abode. It was a blessed interval. During that period of rest the longing for solitude came over
him; a longing which he never lost during all the remainder
of his active days. He was still Augustine, the half-pagan;
the saint was yet to be formed. The love of argument still
delighted him, and that in surroundings that made life on
earth most sweet; the comforts of ease, the pleasure of con-
genial companions, the delight in everything that his eyes
could gaze upon. If he laid aside his lectures in Milan, none
the less he went on teaching in his new home; but his lessons were drawn from the good things about him, the light
in the sky at dawn, the noise of running waters, the goodly

warmth of the sun in his veins. By means such as these the natural man was clarified, prepared for the great things that were yet to come.

That he might begin again he must leave Milan and Rome, and return to his native Thagaste. On the way his party stopped at Ostia; there took place the memorable scene which he shared with his mother, Monica, when, as he tells us, her conversation led him up to a vision of God he had never known before; there, too, his mother died, and the loss almost broke his heart.

He returned to Carthage and thence quickly made his way to Thagaste. Now he could begin in real earnest; and he began as he had learned others had begun before him. His inheritance, now that his mother was dead, he distributed to the poor; for himself, he would turn his house into a monastery, and with his friends, would live a life of prayer, and study, and retirement. But this was not to be. Already he was famous in Thagaste; and there came a day when, as was the manner of those times, the people would have him for their priest and he was ordained. As a priest he was sent to Hippo, and there his new career began. He lived a monastic life, but his learning and preaching, first to his own people, then against the heretics about him, made it impossible that he should be hid; soon the cry was raised that he should be the bishop.

The rest of his story need not concern us; the rout of the Donatists, who then threatened to dominate northern Africa, the rebuilding of the Church in true poverty of spirit, along with care for the poor, and what we would call the working-classes, the administration of the law which fell upon his shoulders, the incessant preaching and writing, the quantity of which at this time appals us. We are. told that he preached every day, sometimes more than once; often enough, as the words of his sermons indicate, his audience would have him continue till he had to dismiss them for their meals. What concerns us more is the inner soul of the man in the midst of all these labours.

For Augustine could never forget what he had been, and

the fear never forsook him that with very little he might be the same again. At the time of his consecration as bishop he asked himself with anxiety whether, with his past, and with the scars from that past still upon him, he could face the burden. From time to time old visions would revive and the passions in his soul would leap towards them; even in his old age he trembled to think that some day they might get the better of him. To suppress temptation he would work without ceasing; he would allow himself no respite. When he was not preaching, or helping other souls, he would write; when he was not writing he would pray. When prayer became blank from utter weariness of age still he would pray with a pen in his hand; the only rest he would allow himself was reading, for that, he confesses, was still his delight. By means such as these he kept his other nature down. When we look at the volumes of his works we may assure ourselves that one at least of the motives which produced them was the determination in Augustine's soul to keep his lower nature in control by incessant labours.

Nevertheless labour alone would never have saved or made the Augustine that we know. Living as he was as archbishop in a time of violence, when knives were easily drawn to solve the problems of theology, he had himself often to act with severity. Still the heart of Augustine was an affectionate heart; if in the old days it had led him far astray, in his later life it led him no less to sanctity. While he mercilessly hammered the Donatists about him, at the same time he could address his fellow priests in words like these:

"Keep this in mind, my brothers; practise it and preach it with meekness that shall never fail. Love the men you fight; kill only their lie. Rest on truth in all humility; defend it but with no cruelty. Pray for those whom you oppose; pray for them while you correct them."

Yet more than that was his ever increasing hunger after God. In the time of his conversion he shows us how this hunger proved his salvation; then he uttered the memorable sentence by which he is best known:

"Thou hast made us, O Lord, for thyself, and our heart shall find no rest till it rest in thee."

As the years went on, and as he grew in understanding of this goal of all affection, the hunger was only the more intensified. There is a pathetic scene recorded in his later life, when he gathered his people about him and complained to them that they would not leave him time to pray. With the simplicity of a child he reminded them that this had been part of the bargain when he had become their bishop; it was their part of the bargain and they had not kept it. He asked them, now that he was growing old, to renew their engagement; to permit him to have some days in the week when he might be alone; then they might do with him what they would. They promised; but again the promise was not kept. Circumstances were against him and them; he was living in an age when the old order was being shaken to its foundations, and there was need of a man to build a new world on its ruins. That man was Augustine, and while his eyes and his heart strained after heaven, his intellect and preaching had perforce to attend to the raising of the City of God.

But it was just for this purpose that Augustine had been made. He knew the pagan world and depicted it as no man has done from his time till now; the picture he draws is as true to-day as it was then. And equally true and efficacious is his antidote. As he himself had to grope through his own darkness till he came to God, and then, and then only, saw all in its right perspective, so he told mankind that they would find no solution of their problems in so-called peace, in shirking all restraint, in substituting law for morality, in stifling every voice that ventured to denounce evil-doing, in finding equivocal phrases which seemed to condone all sin. They would find it only where alone it could be found; the world would find no rest till it found it in God.

Augustine did not live to see so much as the dawn of the new day which he heralded; on the contrary, his sun went down, and there came over Africa and Hippo the blackest night. As the old man sat in his palace the news was brought to him of the wanton destruction carried out by the Arian Vandals. Nothing was being spared; to this day Northern Africa has not recovered from the scourge. The word *vandalism* passed into the language of Europe at that time, and has never since been superseded. He heard it all, he appealed to the Roman ruler to defend the right; he was listened to, and then he was betrayed. Still he did not move. With energy he called on his priests to stay with their flocks, and if need be to die with them. At length came the turn for Hippo to be besieged by land and sea. In the third month of the siege Augustine fell ill, probably of one of the fevers which a siege engenders. He grew worse; he knew he was dying; he made a general confession and then, at last, asked that he might be left alone with God. Lying on his bed he heard the din of battle in the distance, and as his mind began to wander he asked himself whether the end of the world had come. But he quickly recovered. No; it was not that. Had not Christ said: "I am with you always, even to the end of the world"? Some day, somehow, the world would be saved. "Non tollit Gothus quod custodit Christus," he told himself, and with this certain hope for mankind he went away to the home he had once described as the place "where we are at rest, where we see as we are seen, where we love and are loved." It was the fifth day of the Calends of September, August 28th, 430.

ST. MARGARET OF CORTONA
THE SECOND MAGDALENE

1247–1297

They were stirring times in Tuscany when Margaret was born. They were the days of Manfred and Conradin, of the Guelphs and Ghibellines in Italy, when passions of every kind ran high, and men lived at great extremes. They were times of great sinners, but also of great saints; Margaret lived to hear of the crowning and resignation of St. Celestine V, whose life and death are a vivid commentary on the spirits that raged throughout that generation. It was the age of St. Thomas in Paris, of Dante in Florence; of Cimabue and Giotto; of the great cathedrals and universities. In Tuscany itself, apart from the coming and going of soldiers, now of the Emperor, now of the Pope, keeping the countryside in a constant state of turmoil, and teaching the country-folk their ways, there were for ever rising little wars among the little cities themselves, which were exciting and disturbing enough. For instance, when Margaret was a child, the diocese in which she lived, Chiusi, owned a precious relic, the ring of the Blessed Virgin Mary. An Augustinian friar got possession of this relic, and carried it off to Perugia. This caused a war; Chiusi and Perugia fought for the treasure and Perugia won. Such was the spirit of her time, and of the people among whom she was brought up.

It was also a time of the great revival; when the new

religious orders had begun to make their mark, and the old ones had renewed their strength. Franciscans and Dominicians had reached down to the people, and every town and village in the country had responded to their call to better things. St. Francis of Assisi had received the stigmata on Mount Alverno twenty years before, quite close to where Margaret was born; St. Clare died not far away, when Margaret was four years old. And there was the opposite extreme, the enthusiasts whose devotion degenerated into heresy. When Margaret was ten there arose in her own district the Flagellants, whose processions of men, women, and children, stripped to the waist and scourging themselves to blood, must have been a not uncommon sight to her and her young companions.

Margaret was born in Laviano, a little town in the diocese of Chiusi. Her parents were working people of the place; their child was very beautiful, and in their devotion, for she was the only one, they could scarcely help but spoil her. Thus from the first Margaret, as we would say, had much against her; she grew up very wilful and, like most spoilt children, very restless and dissatisfied. Very soon her father's cottage was too small for her; she needed companions; she found more life and excitement in the streets of the town. Next, in course of time the little town itself grew too small; there was a big world beyond about which she came to know, and Margaret longed to have a part in it. Moreover she soon learnt that she could have a part in it if she chose. For men took notice of her, not only men of her own station and surroundings, whom she could bend to her will as she pleased; but great and wealthy men from outside, who would sometimes ride through the village, and notice her, and twit her for her beautiful face. They would come again; they were glad to make her acquaintance, and sought to win her favour. Margaret quickly learned that she had only to command, and there were many ready to obey.

While she was yet very young her mother died; an event which seemed to deprive her of the only influence that had hitherto held her in check. Margaret records that she was taught by her mother a prayer she never forgot: "O Lord Jesus, I beseech thee, grant salvation to all those for whom thou wouldst have me pray." To make matters worse her father married again. He was a man of moods, at one time weak and indulgent, at another violent to excess, and yet with much in him that was lovable, as we shall have reason to see. But with the step-mother there was open and continued conflict. She was shocked at Margaret's wilfulness and independence, and from her first coming to the house was determined to deal with them severely. Such treatment was fatal to Margaret. As a modern student has written of her: "Margaret's surroundings were such as to force to the surface the weaknesses of her character. As is clear from her own confessions, she was by nature one of those women who thirst for affection; in whom to be loved is the imperative need of their lives. She needed to be loved that her soul might be free, and in her home she found not what she wanted. Had she been of the weaker sort, either morally or physically, she would have accepted her lot, vegetated in spiritual barrenness, married eventually a husband of her father's choice, and lived an uneventful life with a measure of peace."

As it was she became only the more wilful and reckless. If there was not happiness for her, either at home or elsewhere, there was pleasure and, with a little yielding on her part, as much of it as she would. In no long time her reputation in the town was one not to be envied; before she was seventeen years of age she had given herself up to a life of indulgence, let the consequences be what they might.

Living such a life it soon became evident that Margaret could not stay in Laviano. The circumstances which took her away are not very clear; we choose those which seem the most satisfactory. A certain nobleman, living out beyond Montepulciano, which in those days was far away, was in need of a servant in his castle. Margaret got the situation; there at least she was free from her step-mother and, within limits, could live as she pleased. But her master

was young, and a sporting man, and no better than others
of his kind. He could not fail to take notice of the handsome girl who went about his mansion, holding her head
high as if she scorned the opinions of men, with an air of
independence that seemed to belong to one above her station. He paid her attention; he made her nice presents; he
would do her kindnesses even while she served him. And
on her side, Margaret was skilled in her art; she was quick
to discover that her master was as susceptible to her influence as were the other less distinguished men with whom
she had done as she would in Laviano. Moreover this time
she was herself attracted; she knew that this man loved her,
and she returned it in her way. There were no other com-
petitors in the field to distract her; there was no mother
to warn her, no step-mother to abuse her. Soon Margaret
found herself installed in the castle, not as her master's
wife, for convention would never allow that, but as his mis-
tress, which was more easily condoned. Some day, he had
promised her, they would be married, but the day never
came. A child was born, and with that Margaret settled
down to the situation.

For some years she accepted her lot, though every day
what she had done grew upon her more and more. Apart
from the evil life she was living, her liberty-loving nature
soon found that instead of freedom she had secured only
slavery. The restless early days in Laviano seemed, in her
present perspective, less unhappy than she had thought;
the poverty and restraint of her father's cottage seemed
preferable to the wealth and chains of gold she now endured. In her lonely hours, and they were many, the memory of her mother came up before her, and she could not
look her shadow in the face. And with that revived the
consciousness of sin, which of late she had defied, and had
crushed down by sheer reckless living, but which now
loomed up before her like a haunting ghost. She saw it all,
she hated it all, she hated herself because of it, but there
was no escape. It was all misery, but she must endure it;
she had made her own bed, and must henceforth lie upon

it. In her solitary moments she would wander into the gloom of the forest, and there would dream of the life that might have been, a life of virtue and of the love of God. At her castle gate she would be bountiful; if she could not be happy herself, at least she could do something to help others. But for the rest she was defiant. She went about her castle with the airs of an unbeaten queen. None should know, not even the man who owned her, the agony that gnawed at her heart. From time to time there would come across her path those who had pity for her. They would try to speak to her; they would warn her of the risk she was running; but Margaret, with her every ready wit, would laugh at their warnings and tell them that some day she would be a saint.

So things went on for nine years, till Margaret was twenty-seven. On a sudden there came an awakening. It chanced that her lord had to go away on a distant journey; in a few days, when the time arrived for his return, he did not appear. Instead there turned up at the castle gate his favourite hound, which he had taken with him. As soon as it had been given admittance it ran straight to Margaret's room, and there began to whine about her, and to tug at her dress as if it would drag her out of the room. Margaret saw that something was amiss.

Anxious, not daring to express to herself her own suspicions, she rose and followed the hound wherever it might lead; it drew her away down to a forest a little distance from the castle walls. At a point where a heap of faggots had been piled, apparently by wood-cutters, the hound stood still, whining more than ever, and poking beneath the faggots with its nose. Margaret, all trembling, set to work to pull the heaps away; in a hole beneath lay the corpse of her lord, evidently some days dead, for the maggots and worms had already begun their work upon it.

How he had come to his death was never known; after all, in those days of high passions, and family feuds, such murders were not uncommon. The careful way the body had been buried suggested foul play; that was all. But for

Margaret the sight she saw was of something more than death. The old faith within her still lived, as we have already seen, and now insisted on asking questions. The body of the man she had loved and served was lying there before her, but what had become of his soul? If it had been condemned, and was now in hell, who was, in great part at least, responsible for its condemnation? Others might have murdered his body, but she had done infinitely worse. Moreover there was herself to consider. She had known how, in the days past, she had stirred the rivalry and mutual hatred of men on her account and had gloried in it; who knew but that this deed had been done by some rival because of her? Or again, her body might have been lying there where his now lay, her fatal beauty being eaten by worms, and in that case where would her soul then have been? Of that she could have no sort of doubt. Her whole life came up before her, crying out now against her as she had never before permitted it to cry. Margaret rushed from the spot, beside herself in this double misery, back to her room, turned in an instant to a torture-chamber.

What should she do next? She was not long undecided. Though the castle might still be her home, she would not stay in it a moment longer. But where could she go? There was only one place of refuge that she knew, only one person in the world who was likely to have pity on her. Though her father's house had been disgraced in the eyes of all the village by what she had done, though the old man all these years had been bent beneath the shame she had brought upon him, still there was the memory of past kindness and love which he had always shown her. It was true sometimes he had been angry, especially when others had roused him against her and her ways; but always in the end, when she had gone to him, he had forgiven her and taken her back. She would arise and go to her father, and would ask him to forgive her once more; this time in her heart she knew she was in earnest—even if he failed her she would not turn back. Clothed as she was, holding her child in her arms, taking no heed of the spectacle she made, she left the castle, tramped over the ridge and down the valley to Laviano, came to her father's cottage, found him within alone and fell at his feet, confessing her guilt, imploring him with tears to give her shelter once again.

The old man easily recognised his daughter. The years of absence, the fine clothes she wore, the length of years which in some ways had only deepened the striking lines of her handsome face, could not take from his heart the picture of the child of whom once he had been so proud. To forgive was easy; it was easy to find reasons in abundance. Had he not indulged her in the early days, perhaps she would never have fallen. Had he made home a more satisfying place for a child of so yearning a nature, perhaps she would never have gone away. Had he been a more careful guardian, had he protected her from those who had lured her into evil ways long ago, she would never have wandered so far, she would never have brought this shame upon him and upon herself. She was repentant, she wished to make amends, she had proved it by this renunciation, she showed she loved and trusted him; he must give her a chance to recover. If he did not give it to her, who would?

So the old man argued with himself, and for a time his counsel prevailed. Margaret with her child was taken back; if she would live quietly at home the past might be lived down. But such was not according to Margaret's nature. She did not wish the past to be forgotten, it must be atoned. She had done great evil, she had given great scandal; she must prove to God and man that she had broken with the past, and that she meant to make amends. The spirit of fighting sin by public penance was in the air; the Dominican and Franciscan missionaries preached it, there were some in her neighbourhood who were carrying it to a dangerous extreme. Margaret would let all the neighbours see that she did not shirk the shame that was her due. Every time she appeared in the church it was with a rope of penance round her waist; she would kneel at the church door that all might pass her by and despise her; since this did not win for her the scorn she desired, one day, when

the people were gathered for mass, she stood up before
the whole congregation and made public confession of the
wickedness of her life.

But this did not please her old father. He had hoped she
would lie quiet and let the scandal die; instead she kept
the memory of it always alive. He had expected that soon
all would be forgotten; instead she made of herself a public
show. In a very short time his mind towards her changed.
Indulgence turned to resentment, resentment to bitterness,
bitterness to something like hatred. Besides, there was another in the house to be reckoned with; the step-mother,
who from her first coming there had never been a friend
of Margaret. She had endured her return because, for the
moment, the old man would not be contradicted; but she
had bided her time. Now when he wavered she brought
her guns to bear; to the old man in secret, to Margaret
before her face, she did not hesitate to use every argument
she knew. This hussy who had shamed them all in the
sight of the whole village had dared to cross her spotless
threshold, and that with a baggage of a child in her arms.
How often when she was a girl had she been warned where
her reckless life would lead her! When she had gone away,
in spite of every appeal, she had been told clearly enough
what would be her end. All these years she had continued,
never once relenting, never giving them a sign of recognition, knowing very well the disgrace she had brought upon
them, while she enjoyed herself in luxury and ease. Let
her look to it; let her take the consequences. That house
had been shamed enough; it should not be shamed any
more, by keeping such a creature under its roof. One day,
when things had reached a climax, without a word of pity
Margaret and her child were driven out of the door. If she
wished to do penance, let her go and join the fanatical
Flagellants, who were making such a show of themselves
not far away.

Margaret stood in the street, homeless, condemned by
her own, an outcast. Those in the town looked on and did
nothing; she was not one of the kind to whom it was either

wise or safe to show pity, much less to take her into their own homes. And Margaret knew it; since her own father had rejected her she could appeal to no one else; she could only hide her head in shame, and find refuge in loneliness in the open lane. But what should she do next? For she had not only herself to care for; there was also the child in her arms. As she sat beneath a tree looking away from Laviano, her eyes wandered up the ridge on which stood Montepulciano. Over that ridge was the bright, gay world she had left, the world without a care, where she had been able to trample scandal underfoot and to live as a queen. There she had friends who loved her; rich friends who had condoned her situation, poor friends who had been beholden to her for the alms she had given them. Up in the castle there were still wealth and luxury waiting for her, and even peace of a kind, if only she would go back to them. Besides, from the castle what good she could do! She was now free; she could repent in silence and apart; with the wealth at her disposal she could help the poor yet more. Since she had determined to change her life, could she not best accomplish it up there, far away from the sight of men?

On the other hand, what was she doing here? She had tried to repent, and all her efforts had only come to this; she was a homeless outcast on the road, with all the world to glare at her as it passed her by. Among her own people, even if in the end she were forgiven and taken back, she could never be the same again. Then came a further thought. She knew herself well by this time. Did she wish that things should be the same again? In Laviano, among the old surroundings which she had long outgrown, among peasants and labourers whom she had long left behind, was it not likely that the old boredom would return, more burdensome now that she had known the delights of freedom? Would not the old temptations return, had they not returned already, had they not been with her all the time, and with all her good intentions was it not certain that she would never be able to resist? Then would her last state be worse than her first. How much better to be prudent, to take the opportunity as it was offered, perhaps to use for good the means and the gifts she had hitherto used only for evil! Thus, resting under a tree in her misery, a great longing came over Margaret, to have done with the penitence which had all gone wrong, to go back to the old life where all had gone well, and would henceforth go better, to solve her problems once and for all by the only way that seemed open to her. That lonely hour beneath the tree was the critical hour of her life.

Happily for her, and for many who have come after her, Margaret survived it: "I have put thee as a burning light," Our Lord said to her later, "to enlighten those who sit in the darkness.—I have set thee as an example to sinners, that in thee they may behold how my mercy awaits the sinner who is willing to repent; for as I have been merciful to thee, so will I be merciful to them." She had made up her mind long ago, and she would not go back now. She shook herself and rose to go; but where? The road down which she went led to Cortona; a voice within her seemed to tell her to go thither. She remembered that at Cortona was a monastery of Franciscans. It was famous all over the countryside; Brother Elias had built it, and had lived and died there; the friars, she knew, were everywhere described as the friends of sinners. She might go to them; perhaps they would have pity on her and find her shelter. But she was not sure. They would know her only too well, for she had long been the talk of the district, even as far as Cortona; was it not too much to expect that the Franciscan friars would so easily believe in so sudden and complete a conversion? Still she could only try; at the worst she could but again be turned into the street, and that would be more endurable from them than the treatment she had just received in Laviano.

Her fears were mistaken. Margaret knocked at the door of the monastery, and the friars did not turn her away. They took pity on her; they accepted her tale though, as was but to be expected, with caution. She made a general confession, with such a flood of tears that those who witnessed it were moved. It was decided that Margaret was, so far at least, sincere and harmless, and they found her a home. They put her in charge of two good matrons of the town, who spent their slender means in helping hard cases and who undertook to provide for her. Under their roof she began in earnest her life of penance. Margaret could not do things by halves; when she had chosen to sin she had defied the world in her sinning, now that she willed to do penance she was equally defiant of what men might think or say. She had revelled in rich clothing and jewels; henceforth, so far as her friends would permit her, she would clothe herself literally in rags. She had slept on luxurious couches; henceforth she would lie only on the hard ground. Her beauty, which had been her ruin, and the ruin of many others besides, and which even now, at twenty-seven, won for her many a glance of admiration as she passed down the street, she was determined to destroy. She cut her face, she injured it with bruises, till men would no longer care to look upon her. Nay, she would go abroad, and where she had sinned most she would make most amends. She would go to Montepulciano; there she would hire a woman to lead her like a beast with a rope round her neck, and cry: "Look at Margaret, the sinner." It needed a strong and wise confessor to keep her within bounds.

Nor was this done only to atone for the past. For years the old cravings were upon her; they had taken deep root and could not at once be rooted out; even to the end of her life she had reason to fear them. Sometimes she would ask herself how long she could continue the fight; sometimes it would be that there was no need, that she should live her life like ordinary mortals. Sometimes again, and this would often come from those about her, it would be suggested to her that all her efforts were only a proof of sheer pride. In many ways we are given to see that with all the sanctity and close union with God which she afterwards attained, Margaret to the end was very human; she was the same

Margaret, however chastened, that she had been at the beginning. "My father," she said to her confessor one day, "do not ask me to give in to this body of mine. I cannot afford it. Between me and my body there must needs be a struggle until death."

The rest of Margaret's life is a wonderful record of the way God deals with his penitents. There were her child and herself to be kept, and the fathers wisely bade her earn her own bread. She began by nursing; soon she confined her nursing to the poor, herself living on alms. She retired to a cottage of her own; here, like St. Francis before her, she made it her rule to give her labour to whoever sought it, and to receive in return whatever they chose to give. In return there grew in her a new understanding of that craving for love which had led her into danger. She saw that it never would be satisfied here on earth; she must have more than this world could give her or none at all. And here God was good to her. He gave her an intimate knowledge of Himself; we might say He humoured her by letting her realise His love, His care, His watchfulness over her. With all her fear of herself, which was never far away, she grew in confidence because she knew that now she was loved by one who would not fail her. This became the character of her sanctity, founded on that natural trait which was at once her strength and her weakness.

And it is on this account, more than on account of the mere fact that she was a penitent, that she deserves the title of the Second Magdalene. Of the first Magdalene we know this, that she was an intense human being, seeking her own fulfilment at extremes, now in sin, now in repentance regardless of what men might think, uniting love and sorrow so closely that she is forgiven, not for her sorrow so much as for her love. We know that ever afterwards it was the same; the thought of her sin never kept her from her Lord, the knowledge of His love drew her ever closer to Him, till, after Calvary, she is honoured the first among those to whom He would show Himself alone. And in that memorable scene we have the two traits which sum her up; He reveals Himself by calling her by her name: "Mary," and yet, when she would cling about His feet, as she had done long before, He bids her not to touch Him. In Margaret of Cortona the character, and the treatment, are parallel. She did not forget what she had been; but from the first the thought of this never for a moment kept her from Our Lord. She gave herself to penance, but the motive of her penance, as her revelations show, was love more than atonement. In her extremes of penance she had no regard for the opinions of men; she would brave any obstacle that she might draw the nearer to Him. At first He humoured her; He drew her by revealing to her His appreciation of her love; He even condescended so far as to call her "Child," when she had grown tired of being called "*Poverella*." But later, when the time for the greatest graces came, then He took her higher by seeming to draw more apart; it was the scene of *Noli me tangere* repeated.

This must suffice for an account of the wonderful graces and revelations that were poured out on Margaret during the last twenty-three years of her life. She came to Cortona as a penitent when she was twenty-seven. For three years the Franciscan fathers kept her on her trial, before they would admit her to the Third Order of St. Francis. She submitted to the condition; during that time she earned her bread, entirely in the service of others. Then she declined to earn it; while she laboured in service no less, she would take in return only what was given to her in alms. Soon even this did not satisfy her; she was not content till the half of what was given her in charity was shared with others who seemed to her more needy. Then out of this there grew other things, for Margaret had a practical and organising mind. She founded institutions of charity, she established an institution of ladies who would spend themselves in the service of the poor and suffering. She took a large part in the keeping of order in that turbulent countryside; even her warlike bishop was compelled to listen to her, and to surrender much of his plunder at her bidding. Like St. Catherine of Siena after her, Margaret is a wonderful instance, not only of the mystic combined with the soul of action, but more of the soul made one of action because it was a mystic, and by means of its mystical insight.

Margaret died in 1297, being just fifty years of age. Her confessor and first biographer tells us that one day, shortly before her death, she had a vision of St. Mary Magdalene, "most faithful of Christ's apostles, clothed in a robe as it were of silver, and crowned with a crown of precious gems, and surrounded by the holy angels." And whilst she was in this ecstasy Christ spoke to Margaret, saying: "My Eternal Father said of Me to the Baptist: This is My beloved Son; so do I say to thee of Magdalene: This is my beloved daughter." On another occasion we are told that "she was taken in spirit to the feet of Christ, which she washed with her tears as did Magdalene of old; and as she wiped His feet she desired greatly to behold His face, and prayed to the Lord to grant her this favour." Thus to the end we see she was the same; and yet the difference!

They buried her in the church of St. Basil in Cortona. Around her body, and later at her tomb, her confessor tells us that so many miracles, physical and spiritual, were worked that he could fill a volume with the record of those which he personally knew alone. And to-day Cortona boasts of nothing more sacred or more treasured than that same body, which lies there still incorrupt, after more than six centuries, for everyone to see.

ST. JOHN OF GOD
THE WAIF

1495–1550

Few people in this world who have made any name for themselves in any sphere began life under such adverse conditions as did St. John of God. He was born in Montemayor-el-Novo, in Portugal, in 1495. His parents were respectable, but not of the richest class; they looked upon their only son as the chief treasure they possessed. But they were not to possess him long. One day, when John was eight years of age, he disappeared. Whether he had been deliberately kidnapped, or whether he had been seduced from his home by some enticing stranger, is not clear; at all events a short time after he found himself an outcast, a homeless waif, in the streets of Oropesa, in the kingdom of Castile, on the opposite coast of the Spanish peninsula from the place where he was born. There, in a foreign land, he had no one to care for him, nothing on which to live; he had to be content with whatever means of subsistence he could find, and he settled down as a shepherd-boy on the neighbouring countryside.

He remained in this solitary life till he was twenty-two years of age; during all that time there seems to be nothing to record about him. Then came a change. It was an age of wars and conquests; and even country villagers, especially in Spain, when the day's work was over, could talk of little else but the new countries being discovered, the great battles being fought, the wonderful deeds being done, by the heroes of the time, from the Emperor-king, Charles V, known among themselves as Charles I, to the common soldier. Men would come home from the wars, and would fire them with marvellous tales, which lost nothing in the telling; voyagers would return from their wanderings across the seas, and would describe the strange people they had met, and the strange sights they had seen, in America or in the Indies. Occasionally one would come back with his pockets apparently full of gold, and would build his own house and settle down at home, independent for the rest of his life; and many a country-bred youth would tell himself that the same could be his if only he would go and do likewise. Then would follow some recruiting officer, who would dangle before these young men's eyes the glittering bait of service in the Emperor's armies; and many would lay aside their ploughs, or leave their sheep on the hillside, to go after the drum of the sergeant and enlist as soldiers.

In the course of time John the shepherd caught the fever like others. When he was about twenty-two years of age he joined a company of foot-soldiers, and in that company fought for the Emperor, Charles V, first against the French in Fontarabia, later in Hungary against the Turks. For some eighteen years John was a trooper employed in various parts of Europe. But while helping to win battles, he lost almost everything else. On the hillsides of Castile he had preserved some practice of religion; now he lost what little of faith and devotion he once possessed. He laid aside his morals; he was ashamed to be thought better than the comrades-in-arms about him; in the course of years John became as hardened in body and soul as anybody else.

Still, not quite everything was gone. Sometimes, when he lay alone on his bed of straw at night, memories of his childhood would come back to him. Though he had been taken from his home at the age of eight, he never forgot the pictures of his early days. The cottage in which he had lived as a child with a contented father and mother would rise up out of the mist; or again the hillsides with the sheep, where he had wandered many a day, all alone, but light-hearted and utterly free. These recollections he would contrast with the life he was living; with the noise and confusion of it all, the wealth that occasionally came from loot, but as quickly disappeared, the revelry and drink and sin, above all the cruelty. Here indeed was a trait which he never lost. However wild his life, John had always a weak spot in his heart for the poor and suffering; however reckless his behaviour, no beggar ever came to John but got relief, if he was able to give it. The trait is not uncommon in men of his kind, as anyone will know who has had to deal with them.

One or two events contributed to deepen these reflections. Once when he was out on a looting expedition he fell from his horse, was severely injured, and narrowly escaped being taken by the enemy. As he lay on the ground expecting death, instinctively the prayers of his childhood came to his lips. He appealed to Mary to save him, and somehow he was rescued. On another occasion he was set to guard an enormous heap of booty. When he was relieved it was found that much of the treasure had been rifled. Naturally the suspicion fell on John; even if he had not been partner in the theft, at least he had failed in his duty. He was condemned to be shot; and that would have been his doom had not some more tolerant officer intervened to win his pardon. Experiences such as these strengthened his disgust for the army; he determined to be rid of it as soon as he could, and to return to the peace he had known.

John was over forty years of age before his day of freedom came. After the campaign in Hungary his regiment was at last disbanded, and the men were landed on the coast of Galicia. Immediately he set about making something of himself; and since in those times it was usual for penitents to begin by being pilgrims, John made a pilgrimage on foot to St. James of Compostella. At the shrine, as became a true pilgrim, he put himself right before God; he made his confession, and determined that in some way the rest of his life should be spent in atonement. With the joy of forgiveness came thoughts of his early childhood, and with them a great longing to know what had become of his family. He accordingly went into Portugal, to the town where he was born; he found there an uncle, to whom he contrived to make himself known. From him he learnt that his mother had died long years ago, partly of a broken heart because of the loss of her son; after her death his father had entered a Franciscan monastery, and there had ended his days. As may well be imagined, this discovery made a deep impression on John, especially at this moment. He looked upon himself, not only as a reprobate trooper, but as having been in some way the cause of his mother's and his father's death, and therefore unfit to live in their country any longer.

John accordingly left Portugal, and returned once more to Spain. But to what could he turn for a means of livelihood? An ex-soldier, at the best of times, was always an object of suspicion among self-respecting citizens. Such a man had been accustomed to a lawless life; he was not overscrupulous about the things that belonged to others; usually he knew no trade, and was too old and unwilling to learn one; his behaviour and language were no good example to the young men and women about him; altogether, prudent fathers and careful mothers had no wish to have him as a member of their establishments. When, then, John sought employment, he only fared like others of his kind. He had nothing to recommend him; his age was a further obstacle; he was miserably poor; in the end he counted himself fortunate to find a situation as a shepherd once more, in the service of a wealthy and benevolent lady who lived near Seville.

Thus at the age of forty-two, John began again where he had left off twenty years before. But now he was a very different man. In his hours of solitude on the hills with his sheep he set himself at least to try to pray; during his prayer it came upon him more than ever what a wasted life he had lived. Indeed it had been more than wasted; he was appalled at the amount of harm he had done to others. There were only two conclusions to be drawn. On the one hand, if he received his rights from men, he would certainly deserve from them nothing but contempt; on the other hand, he who had done so much harm, who stood responsible for the lives of so many, perhaps his mother included, could never be content to remain in comparative ease among his sheep. In some way he must give what remained of his life in atonement for the lives of those he had ruined; he must do some good to balance the harm.

What should he do? He would take the first thing that came his way. There was much talk at the time of the sufferings of Christian slaves among the Moors of Africa. He would go over to them; if he could get money he would spend it all in their ransom; if he could not, then perhaps he could substitute himself for one of them. With this plan in his mind, John gave up his shepherd's life and made his way to Gibraltar. Here he came across a Portuguese who for some reason had been exiled from his country, and was about to settle with his family across the strait at Ceuta. He was utterly destitute; this decided John to go with him, and at least to begin by serving him. They came to Ceuta; there John found work on the fortifications which were being built, handing over his earnings to his destitute fellow countryman.

But this did not last long. In a very short time a priest who worked in the settlement discovered him. When he learnt something more of his new parishioner and his past, he spared no pains to persuade John to return to Spain; Africa was no place for men like him. He pointed out to him the risk he ran by living in his present surroundings. In part they were too like those of his old days; his companions were not dissimilar, soon the old temptations would return and he would fall. There was the added danger of association with Mohammedans. Already some of his kind had joined their sect, lured by their moral code, which suited their fancy better than their own; if John was not careful he would follow them, and his last case would be worse than his first.

John listened to the warning of the priest and returned to Spain. He had failed in his first attempt, but he was in no way discouraged. He had made up his mind to spend his life in the two things we have seen, securing for himself the kind of justice he deserved, and somehow doing good to others; how these things were brought about mattered very little. Soon he invented for himself a trade which served his purpose very well. We next hear of him going from village to village, with a wheelbarrow or a hawker's basket, selling pious pictures and religious books and objects of devotion to anyone who would buy; when he found a customer he did not part with his wares till he had given him, over and above, an exhortation to use his purchase well and be good. In this manner he came to Granada. While on this journey, tradition tells us that he found a small child on the roadside, ill-clad and barefooted, who asked John to carry him part of his way. Without more ado John lifted the child on his shoulders, and trudged along with his double burden. But the weight was heavy, and John was none too strong; when he reached a drinking fountain on the road John proposed to the child that they should stop and rest. The child came down from his shoulders but was suddenly transformed. "John of God," he said, "Granada shall be your cross," and immediately disappeared.

Arrived at Granada, John continued the trade he had chosen for himself, but on a larger scale; if he could not preach, or help souls by any powers of his own, at least he could do good by such means as this. He rented a shop at a street corner near the city gate, and there continued to sell his pictures, books and pious objects. He was also a constant visitor at the neighbouring church. Now it chanced that a preacher at that church was Blessed John of Avila, the friend of St. Teresa, of St. Francis Borgia, and of others well known for their sanctity. One day (it was the feast of St. Sebastian, a great day in Spain) John of Avila was preaching; he had taken for his subject the glory of being made a fool for the sake of Jesus Christ. John of God was among his hearers; during the sermon it struck him that here was an obvious and simple solution of his first problem, that of making people treat him as his past life deserved. If he could do nothing else at least he could do this; if he could be nothing else at least he could be a fool. No sooner was the sermon over than he set to work. As the congregation poured out into the street, John went before, crying out for mercy, tearing his hair, beating himself on face and body, rolling in the mud, sitting on the pavement at the feet of the passers-by. So he moved from street to street, amid the ridicule of the neighbours, and to the intense amusement of the children who followed him in crowds. The more they laughed the more John persisted in his folly; he played his part to perfection. Soon the neighbours were convinced that the keeper of the shop at the corner of the street was of unsound mind. He had always been queer, so they said, now they saw that he had fits of insanity, and they began to be sorry for him.

But John was far from being content with their pity; he must be treated as a madman or all his efforts would be in vain. Accordingly on another day, when service was about to begin in the church, John rushed in, threw himself on the ground, and began again to cry out for mercy, louder than ever before. Of course there was a commotion; it was now quite clear that he was mad, and had become a public nuisance. Some pious members of the congregation took hold of him, and carried him off forthwith to the nearest lunatic asylum. At last John had got his wish; he was really taken for a fool, and was to be treated accordingly; to assure himself that this treatment should continue, in his prison he began to play the lunatic more than ever. Now in those days the chief cure for lunacy was the whip. John therefore, as a particularly troublesome patient, was taken out every day and scourged; but the more his keepers scourged him, the more did John persist in his folly.

At length one day what was going on reached the ears

of Blessed John of Avila. Now Blessed John, probably through the confessional, had come to know the shopkeeper a little; and though he easily allowed that he might be what men would call eccentric, he was certainly not mad nor in any sense a lunatic. Hence he was not slow to guess his penitent's manœuvre, and determined to put an end to it. He went to the hospital, and asked to see John alone. Then he gave him a sound scolding. He pointed out to John that he was untruthful; he was pretending to be mad whereas he was quite sane. He was unjust; he was living on the alms intended for lunatics, while he was quite able to look after himself. He was wanting in charity; for he was giving endless trouble to everyone about him, though he had resolved to spend himself in their service. All this made John see his folly in a new light. He became immediately sane, and Blessed John of Avila was soon able to secure him his release; possibly some may have thought that he had worked a miracle.

John came away from his prison, and again betook himself to his little shop. But by this time, as the lunatic episode proves, it had grown too small for his zeal and his energies; he could not wait all day for good people to come to him, he must find something else to do. First he went on a pilgrimage to Our Lady of Guadaloupe, and apparently came back with his mind made up; at last it would seem, after all these years, he had discovered his true vocation. He came back to Granada, rented another house, and immediately began to gather in it all the refuse inhabitants of the town. It did not seem to matter who they were; homeless tramps and vagabonds, cripples begging at church doors, the poor in the streets wherever he might find them, prisoners let out of gaol, all seemed the same to John; he invited them all to his house so long as there was a board on which they might lie. Often enough, when he found on the road beggars too deformed to be able to crawl to his lodging, he hoisted them upon his back and carried them there himself; John with such a load became a familiar sight in the streets of Granada.

Within the house John did all the work himself. He had at first no servants, no nurses; his experience in the wars now stood him in good stead, for there his natural charity had taught him something about wounds and bandages. So he set to work with the little he knew. He could wash his patients and dress their sores; he could kiss their feet and let them feel that somebody cared; he could put them to bed and give them a sense of home; he could sit by their side and be merry with them, and then could induce them to go to confession and pray; it was all very rough and ready, but it suited his household. Under such management it was wonderful how this gathering of the refuse of Granada soon became a model of quiet and content. At first the neighbours resented his conduct; in no long time they were glad to let John go his own way. For the maintenance of his establishment he went out to beg. He had been a hawker and had learnt how to use his voice in the streets; moreover, with his keen sense of humour, he had discovered ways to induce men and women to buy his wares. He made use of the same methods now. He went about the town, rattling a tin can in his hand, shouting as loud as charity could make him, and the burden of his cry showed that his humour had not deserted him. "Do yourselves a good turn, ladies and gentleman, do yourselves a good turn," was the form of appeal he adopted; and its novelty made his hearers laugh, but it also induced them to open their purses. Money began to come in by this single channel; very soon those who gave John alms followed him to see what he did with it. Their eyes were opened; they were astonished to discover what a single man could do unaided, and a man without any qualifications whatsoever. He was neither nurse nor doctor, neither priest nor religious, his education was virtually none, he had no one to help him except his own patients, who occasionally caught the fever of his charity. Very soon there grew up about his house a group of more wealthy men and women who took pride in calling themselves his benefactors.

Thus in an incredibly short time John found himself a

kind of public character in Granada. He rose to the situation. On the one side he accepted any means that was likely to help him in the service of stricken humanity, on the other side his net was extended so as to include every type of outcast. He was not content with gathering up the beggars off the streets; he went and searched them out in the hovels in which they lived. Even houses of ill fame were the object of his raids; indeed it is clear that they soon became a matter for his special concern. He went in among them, scolded and exhorted and sympathised with those who lived in them, as often as not was only laughed at for his pains, but in return brought away many a penitent and set her up in an honest way of life.

Meanwhile the work he was doing attracted the notice of the ecclesiastical authorities. There were those who were suspicious, who had little faith in such freakish ways; there were others who could not but see the astonishing fruit of John's work. He was called to meet the bishop, who also at the time held the post of Mayor of Granada. The bishop asked him his name; John replied that once upon a time a child he had helped in a country lane had called him John of God.

"Then John of God shall be your name always," the bishop answered, and this was how he came to have the title. Then the bishop asked him about his dress. For John, even in this august company, presented a sad appearance; he was wearing a suit of clothes he had taken from a beggar in exchange for his own. The bishop bade him wear a habit; by this dress it would be clear to all that he acted with the bishop's approval. The next step was a hospital proper which the citizens of Granada gave him; and by a hospital we must understand a kind of workhouse, though even a workhouse, as we now interpret it, would be much too good a name. Henceforward John had to give himself to administration; he had a staff of volunteers who worked under his direction, many of them men whom he had rescued from misfortune, who were ready to make amends in the way he showed them.

But John could never have been a saint had he merely prospered; prosperity alone never makes a saint. Besides a few friends, he had many enemies; the kind of work he did almost inevitably provoked opposition. First were the outsiders, who looked on from a distance. They denounced this excessive consideration for the outcast; such treatment as John gave them could only encourage vagabonds and idlers in their evil ways. There were others who put him on his trial for the misuse and squandering of the moneys entrusted to him; practically he was accused of embezzlement. Often enough, it must be confessed, there seemed to be justice on their side; for John did not keep accounts, and money slipped through his fingers as quickly as it came. For instance, once when he went to Valladolid to beg from the court established there, he came away with a large sum of money, but arrived at Granada without any. He had given it all away on the road, chiefly in Valladolid itself; and when his friends at home blamed him for having come back empty-handed he would only say:

"God is in Valladolid as well as in Granada, and we can give to Him there as well as here."

Again, there were many, young and old, who never forgot that he had once been an inmate of a lunatic asylum, and treated him accordingly. Once a boy met him, carrying a bucket of dirty water. He poured the contents over John the lunatic; whereupon all in the street burst into laughter. But John burst into laughter with them; which made some think him only a greater fool, while others thought him a saint. Another time John's cloak accidentally brushed against a Spanish gentleman, and fell to the ground at his feet. The gentleman was indignant, and dealt John a staggering blow. John recovered himself, picked up his cloak, and then stood before his assailant for another.

But these were only the outside trials which signified nothing to John and troubled him very little; what affected him more were the persecutions coming from inside the hospital. There were the many quarrels among the patients themselves, almost inevitable when we consider who they were; and John, in his efforts to be peacemaker, came in for blame from many sides. They would denounce him for injustice, or extravagance, or something else; there were times when it seemed that all his labours had come to nothing. Most troublesome of all were the women whom he had rescued from a life of sin. He had been more than once warned that to do more for these poor creatures than to take them from their evil surroundings was dangerous. They were treacherous by nature, they were ungrateful, they were notoriously unstable, their very repentance, in most cases, was only a pretence; if he did more for them they would only turn upon him. John was well aware that this was only too true; nevertheless he went on as before. He found them a home, as we have already seen he procured the means to give many of them a new start in life; still it was only to receive in return, for the most part, what his friends had told him would come. In the home he had provided for them these poor, restless creatures were difficult to control. They were never satisfied; no matter what he gave them they always asked for more. They looked upon themselves as something superior to the beggar man about them who had made himself their slave. Abuse was all he deserved, and he received it from them in overflowing. When he could not find for them all they demanded, when he attempted to suggest to them better thoughts than those they had always in their minds, then they would turn on him with ridicule, call him a hypocrite and a bigot, hint to him that he knew too much about their lives to be himself wholly innocent.

And John, with his usual good humour, would take their abuse in good part. It was characteristic of him throughout his life that he never took offence; he knew himself too well for that. He would join in the laughter against himself; he would tell these women that what they said against him must be true. Once when one of them was particularly abusive, raking up his early life against him, he gave her two silver coins that she might go into the street and proclaim to all the world what she had charged him with in private. On another occasion, when a visitor chanced to overhear the abuse that was being poured upon him and wished to interfere, John begged him to leave his accusers alone. "I beg you of your charity," he said, "to let them have their say. They know me better than you, and they know that I am a bad lot, worse than they."

John of God was a saint in a category all his own. He lived his own life without anyone to help him, he grew in sanctity after his own manner, he did his work almost entirely single-handed. The Order which he founded, the Brothers Hospitallers of St. John of God, grew almost without his knowing it; it was the fruit of his example and inspiration, its first members were men whose lives had been akin to his own, and whom he had won to do as he did in atonement. And the divine consolations he received were characteristic of himself. We have mentioned the Child that was so heavy a burden in his early days, when he first made his way to Granada. Once, in later years, as he prayed before a crucifix, he seemed to see before him his Lord, Jesus Christ, Our Lady, and St. John. Our Lady stepped forward from the group with a crown, not of gold, not of roses, but of thorns in her hand, and pressed it hard upon his head. "John," she said, "it is by thorns and sufferings that you must win the crown my Son has waiting for you in heaven." John felt the thorns piercing his very brain; still he could only reply: "From your hand, Lady, thorns and sufferings are welcome; they are my flowers and my roses."

Another time he found a beggar in the street, deserted and apparently dying. As usual he took him upon his shoulders, and carried him to his hospital. There he laid him on a bed, and began to wash his feet. But the feet had gaping wounds in them; John looked up in surprise, and found the beggar had been transfigured. He seemed to be all shining, and the brightness seemed to envelop John himself. When he was again alone, and was walking through the hospital, so brilliant a light shone about him that the sick in the ward took alarm, thinking he was on fire; and John had much difficulty in assuring them that all was well.

So John went through the last fifteen years of his life, keeping his two resolutions, to atone for the harm he had done to others in his early days by doing only good to them now, and by ignoring his own very existence. He gave when he had nothing for himself; when he was ill, which was often, he took no notice of his illness that he might serve others who were worse. But there came a time when he could hold out no longer. One day, when he was out on an errand of charity, he chanced to pass along the riverside, and saw a man in the river drowning. Without more ado he went into the water and saved him, but he came home that evening shivering and in high fever. He struggled on to his ordinary work, but at intervals he was obliged to lie down in his own hospital, alongside of those he called his children. These children took alarm; to do such a thing was unlike their father; they would get out of their beds and crowd around his couch, so that John was in danger of being suffocated. A benefactress came to the rescue. On one of her visits to the hospital she discovered what was going on, and wished to have John taken to some other home where he might be better tended. But John demurred; not until she had been supported by the express order of the bishop would he consent to be removed.

In this way he came to die; when the end seemed certain the bishop himself gave him the last sacraments. Then he was asked whether he had anything on his mind. Yes, he had. His answer was characteristic of the man, the model of practical charity.

"There are three things that make me uneasy," he said. "The first is that I have received so many graces from God, and have not recognised them, and have repaid them with so little of my own. The second is that after I am dead, I fear lest the poor women I have rescued, and the poor sinners I have reclaimed, may be treated badly. The third is that those who have trusted me with money, and whom I have not fully repaid, may suffer loss on my account."

He was reassured on these points and his mind was set at rest. Then, even more characteristically, he requested those round his bed to leave him alone for a few minutes; he had lived his life alone, he would die alone. When they were gone he rose from his bed and knelt before a crucifix. The nurses entered shortly after and found him still kneeling there, his face resting on the feet of the Saviour, but he was quite dead. His body remained kneeling till it was taken up to be laid out for burial. It was the eighth of March, 1550, a little after midnight. At the time of his death John was fifty-five years of age.

THE "FAILURE" OF
ST. FRANCIS XAVIER

1506–1552

Probably there is no saint whose name occurs in the Church's calendar, perhaps there is no hero in history, who has more enthusiastic admirers than St. Francis Xavier. Certainly it would be hard to find more highly coloured panegyrics than those which have been written of him, from his own brethren in France and Spain to our own poet Dryden. The boundless range of his horizon, his life of utter devotedness, the splendid fruit of his labours, all appeal to every man who looks for greatness, and compel him to pay homage. The most materialistic and the most utilitarian, whatever they may think of saints as such, are forced to acknowledge that here, at least, was a man, even while he was a saint. That one should surrender all that Xavier surrendered for the sake of his fellow-men, that he should seem to have known no limits to his giving, or to the people to whom he gave, but perhaps, above all, that he should have succeeded in doing the work he did, all this appeals to the man of action and results, who reckons work done by the price that is paid for it and by the fruit that is reaped. Hence it is that panegyrists, both inside and outside the Church, dwell most of all on this aspect of the saint as that which appeals to every man.

At the same time, one cannot help asking oneself whether as a matter of fact this side of his life is the one which is really most to be admired. One cannot help asking whether St. Francis Xavier himself, were he now in heaven allowed to select, would choose this glorious picture of himself as the one which redounded most to his credit, or as the one he would most bring before men's notice in proof of the manhood that was in him. To anyone who reads between the lines of the story of his life the fact of the other side is only too evident. In his own day, and among his own people, he was by no means the great success we, looking back, can see him to have been. On the contrary, we are not without proofs, both internal and external, that to many at least of his contemporaries he was thought a failure. While here and there he had a few staunch friends, and while his capacity for friendship is manifest in every letter that he wrote, still there is, throughout his life, a certain isolation and loneliness which cannot be mistaken. At times he seems almost to cry out against it; when, for instance, he writes to all his brethren in Europe, saying he would gladly write to each one if he could; when in his moments of distress he addresses a single faithful follower in India; when he leaves all alone and hides himself away to seek the one Friend who, he knows, will never fail him.

Still more evidence have we of his own deep conviction that he was himself of little worth. By nature highly strung and sanguine, he suffered from strong reactions; endowed with talents and gifts beyond the ordinary, he was weighed down with the littleness of men around him, blocking his way at every turn; a man of broad horizons and boundless ambitions, he seemed forever tempted to depression and despair, and to surrender every task he undertook. The real greatness of the man must surely lie in this, that he did what he did in spite of every discouragement, from without and from within, and that he died with his eyes stretched forward to a yet further horizon, counting all he had so far done as nothing, probably counting it a failure.

From the day when he decided to throw in his lot with St. Ignatius he was a disappointment to those who had

hitherto known him. His family was disappointed with
him. It was noble, but now was not rich; it had lost its
all because of its staunch support of the French claim
against the Spanish for the lordship of Navarre: in the campaign which led up to the fall of Pampeluna, his own
brothers had fought on the side of the French victors. Now,
since the reverse, it had done what it could to give this
youngest son a fresh start in life; since he could not serve
under a Spanish conqueror, he should be offered a career
of learning, a career in the Church. Yet here he was, at
the mere instigation of an eccentric beggar-student, and a
Spaniard besides, whose past was more than suspicious,
sacrificing all his prospects, and starting on some wild-
goose chase to convert the Holy Land! It must be confessed that many a more Christian family than even that
of Xavier would have been justified in its disappointment
on a less apparent ground than this.

Again, the University was disappointed with him. It had
given him every advantage; it had appointed him to a pro-
fessorship; it had marked him out for a career which only
needed his own energy to lift him up to the highest rank
of the new élite of Europe. Yet all the return he made
was, in a moment of enthusiasm, to throw it all up at the
suggestion of one who had already come to be looked upon
with reserve. Surely there was ground for the resentment
of the authorities against the intrusion of Iñigo Loyola; and
their judgment that Francis Xavier was, after all, fickle and
light-headed, a dreamer of dreams and unreliable, was not
without a basis of good evidence.

Then to his companions, the first members of the Society of Jesus, his life seemed so arranged, his character so
singular, as constantly to lead to disappointment. In the
enthusiasm of his conversion, he wished to go to the Carthusians, and it needed all the influence of Ignatius to prevent him. On their first tramp to Rome, he had carried
his penance to an excess which any man of judgment might
easily have avoided, and only a miracle prevented him from
becoming a burden to them all. Arrived in Italy, he was

sent to Bologna. There he made his mark; he was a born preacher and apostle; evidently he was the man to reform that and other cities; and he was called away from the midst of it all to sit at a desk, seemingly useless and unknown as a mere private secretary. Nevertheless, here again he succeeded. His brethren saw the wisdom of having such a man at the elbow of their Father General. One so gifted, so far-seeing, so sympathetic, so devoted, would be of untold service in framing the new Constitutions and in directing the fast-growing Order; yet, on a sudden, they found that, at a single day's notice, he had gone away to Portugal, thence to be lost to civilization altogether.

In Portugal again he found his place. There he had to wait for more than six months until the fleet for the Indies was equipped. The time was spent in the apostolate, the spirit of Bologna revived; prisoners in gaol were evangelized, especially the victims of the Inquisition, and even accompanied to the stake. But his chief labour was among the nobles, those whose lives and example counted for so much that was evil, whose conversion would mean so much for the world they ruled. And with these he succeeded. Such a preacher had never been known at Court before; so great a reform had never before been brought about. It would clearly be a mistake that such a good work should be cut short; king, and people, and clergy clamoured that Xavier should be left in Portugal, and another sent to the Indies in his place. It was not for the first time that the report went round concerning him that here was a good man being utterly thrown away.

So many changes in five brief years, and Xavier was already thirty-five. He set sail for India on his birthday, 1541, full of the tales which he heard of the countries awaiting him, white for the harvest, of kings and people who were only too eager to receive the saving religion of the beloved Portuguese. When he arrived he found things very different, though probably he was not surprised. Goa, a city of luxury and slaves, where Europeans vied with Asiatics in every worst vice and excess—this was the base from which he had to work. A people hating a religion which came to them with fire and sword, some inveigled with promises of reward, others compelled to intermarry with Portuguese soldiers and camp-followers—if indeed it may safely be called intermarriage—such were the races "craving" for the waters of baptism. A priesthood of the laxest morals, a convent in which every nun had her serf attendant—such was the material with which he had to work. Churches there were in abundance, standing almost side by side. Sunday, when women and some men were borne to church, and slaves carried their prayer-books by their side, was a day to be seen in Goa. For the rest, religion was chiefly of account as a means to conquest and wealth.

Into such a welter of religion and luxury and tyranny Xavier was thrown, and the first result was only to be expected. He was for ever at war with the Portuguese officials; and that not so much, or not only, because he interfered with their authority, or because he thwarted their cupidity, or because he brought home to them unpleasant truths which they had hoped to have left behind them in Europe, but also because he never seemed to be satisfied with what was given him. He had come to India under the protection of the Portuguese flag; the faith should go with the flag, so they thought, even the best among them, and a people won to the faith was a people won to Portugal. But this restless man was not content with this. Not even the vast expanse of the Portuguese possessions sufficed for him, nor all the money they bestowed on him to succour his starving neophytes. He would go where he chose; he would demand protection and help for work that would bring them no return; though officially sent out by the king of Portugal, he would serve the crown just so far as it pleased him and no more. It cannot be denied that the complaints that went home to Portugal, and even to the General, St. Ignatius, in Rome, were not wholly without foundation, and to one who did not know better must have seemed very convincing indeed.

But while this was the conclusion of some men, not utterly unreasonable as men count reason, a still greater disappointment was felt by the man himself. By nature Francis Xavier was one who lived with high ideals, and who seemed destined to find his only happiness in working for a definite goal. Yet one after another the goal he set before himself was snatched from his grasp. There is evidence to show that as a child he would gladly have followed his brothers in the service of his country; his family could not afford it, and he must make his own way in the world. At the University, beyond a doubt, he revelled in the thought of all that lay before him; the hope must surely have lingered in his mind that his master would bid him win his place as a scholar for the greater glory of God. Instead, he was told to give it all up, and tramp to Rome and take ship for Syria. He did as he was told, and was rewarded by a craving for the life of contemplation. He even doubted, so someone tells us, whether that were not his vocation; instead he was not even allowed the journey to the holy places, but was thrown into the cities of Italy to preach and give instructions.

Again he did as he was told, and again a new ambition lay before him. He could preach, and he knew it; he could teach because he knew what he knew; he would give himself heart and soul to this work, for God, and for man's salvation. He had scarcely begun and caught on, when he was ordered to put it all aside and retire into the hidden life of a private secretary. Still, even here there was something to live for. On the one hand there was the great task of building up a great religious order; on the other was the constant companionship of the one friend of his bosom. Here he could live, and do great work, and be happy; and on a sudden he was told to be ready in a day to depart for Portugal and the Indies, to go out of everything for which he had lived, to go out of life as he knew it altogether.

Here a fact should be remembered which adds to the pathos of the situation. There is no record whatever that Francis Xavier had ever set his heart on the foreign missions, or had ever felt for them any particular vocation. With other saints and great missionaries it was different. St. Peter Claver trained himself for the negroes from the beginning of his so-called conversion. Blessed Charles Spinola looked forward from the first to work among the heathen. The North American missionaries and the missionaries in China were all practically volunteers. With St. Francis Xavier there is no record that it was so. He was simply told to go and he went; all his University ambitions, all his contemplative longings, all his schemes for the good of his Order, were annihilated once and for ever. Humanly speaking, the parting was death; it had not the spring of a young missionary going out to the goal of his desires; and perhaps there were other reasons besides sanctity for the singular silence of the man at the moment of parting, usually so demonstrative, so simple in the expression of his emotions.

When he began his work in India, the same disappointment and failure seemed to dog his steps. Of the few companions he took out with him, not more than one seems to have persevered. The first and daring mission among the natives, where the faith found good soil, was all but swept off the face of the earth by an inroad of heathen invaders. His extraordinary powers as Papal Nuncio, and plenipotentiary of the king of Portugal, were practically never used except against those who thwarted him. It was his failure in the king's dominions that drove him farther afield, to the extreme East, and thence to Japan. More than once he had to complain, so far as he dared, of the poor material that was sent out to help him, poor alike in intellect and in spirit; and one finds him almost beside himself, as he cries out to the men of genius who are wasting their lives, so he calls it, winning themselves renown in the Universities of Europe. As the years wore on, and everything he did seemed to fail, he declared his longing to leave the Indies alone, and to go to Abyssinia, to Arabia, to Madagascar, anywhere so that he might do some little good before he died, for all he had done so far had apparently been brought to nothing. Exhausted in body and soul, he buried himself for weeks at a time in the garden of the College at Goa.

What was this College at Goa? Let us take its story as a key to the inner life of the Apostle of the Indies.

Of all the works Xavier set on foot none was more dear to him than the College of St. Paul. Since he could not hope to have from Europe missionaries of either the number or quality he needed, he determined to make missionaries of his own in India; and that these might be trained uncontaminated, as far as possible, by the life, heathen or Christian, around them, he would bring them up apart, under his own supervision. In other words, the College, which he took over and reconstructed as his own, was to be a nursing home for native priests and catechists, from whatever part of the East they might come. That these might grow up with a spirit of their own, independent of all European contact or subjection, none but pure Asiatics were to be accepted. That such an institution might prosper, it was obvious from the first that it would need a Rector on whom he could rely. In all his service, Xavier had only two such men. One he had been compelled to send south to the Fishery Coast, to control the work he had there set on foot. The other was not a Portuguese; he came from the Netherlands and, knowing the Portuguese, Xavier on that account feared to appoint him.

Accordingly he had written to Europe, asking that a worthy Rector might be sent. Rodriguez, the Provincial, responded, and there arrived in Goa, while Xavier was away in the South, a young Jesuit father, Antonio Gomez, with his letters of appointment as Rector in his pocket. He was duly installed, and at once, both in the College and in the city, things began to stir. Gomez was a devoted disciple of the University of Coimbra. He had made his name there, he knew no other; for him the University, with its life and methods, were the acme of perfection, on whose model all other colleges must be built. He was, besides, an excellent preacher, far more impressive, if one may judge from reports, than Xavier himself. His manners were beyond criticism; he was sought after by the highest people in Goa, from the viceroy and bishop downwards, as a guest in their homes, as a confessor for the fastidious Goan ladies. He had moreover the confidence of his Provincial, Simon Rodriguez, in Europe; the decree for his appointment had been given him without any consultation of Xavier. He was a man of unbounded self-confidence and assurance; besides, having come out some six years later than Francis, he could claim both greater experience in the management of schools, and even a better knowledge of the spirit and working of the Society of Jesus itself.

When, then, he was installed as Rector of the College of St. Paul's, Antonio at once set about his reforms. He began with the brethren, his own religious community. Regulations were drawn up and enforced, concerning eating and drinking, sleeping and recreation, spiritual duties and work, strictly according to the practice of Paris and Coimbra. The conditions of the East were ignored; that the spirit of the Society should be relaxed because of mere climate was unthinkable. He ruled with a rod of iron, as became his notion of a strong superior; should any subject prove recalcitrant, he announced that he had authority to send insubordinates to Portugal, if necessary in chains.

Next, he turned his attention to the students. These undisciplined and mixed young men, coming as they did from various parts of India and the further East, were ordered to conform to the ways and customs of Coimbra. The result was inevitable; in a very short time they began to climb over the college walls and run away. But this troubled the Rector very little. He had other and better designs in view. The College of St. Paul must be raised to the status of a university; only as such would it be worthy of the Society of Jesus. To this end it was essential that European students should be admitted, the sons of the officials and magnates of Goa and of all the Portuguese dominions. Education was all important for such as these, and the labours of the Society would be most profitably spent on their training. Out of these, moreover, far more becoming vocations might be looked for; as for the candidates whom Father Francis had in mind, for them the apostolic schools would suffice, scattered in various places, preferably away from the metropolis of Goa.

Francis on his return saw what was being done; he remonstrated, but to no purpose. Gomez had been sent to teach the Society in the East, Xavier himself included, the ways of the Society in Portugal, not to be taught the ways of a lax and undisciplined community. What was to be done? The crisis had come in the few months Francis had been in Goa between his return from the East Indies and his departure for Japan. All had been arranged for the voyage; if he lost this opportunity he might not find another for a year. To leave all authority in the hands of this man would be fatal; yet on his other expeditions he had always done this with the former Rector. He must give Gomez another appointment. He must send him out of Goa, to Ormuz, to Diu, to Bassein, to one of the Portuguese settlements where his learning and talents would have full scope, and where he would have less opportunity for mischief. In his stead he must run the risk of appointing the one trusty subject he had at hand, the Hollander, Fr. Gaspar Baertz.

So Francis determined, but circumstances were too much for him. Fr. Gaspar saw only too well the difficulties before him, and pleaded to be excused; a Dutch superior would be pleasing neither to the members of the Society nor to the Portuguese authorities. Fr. Antonio on the other hand was aggrieved; he questioned the right of Fr. Francis to override the decision of their common Provincial in Portugal. To strengthen his cause he called in the aid of his friends, the viceroy, the bishop, and others; these expressed surprise that so excellent a man, so exceptional a preacher, so great an influence for good should be removed from the city. In the end, much against his will, but left with little other choice, Xavier was compelled to yield. The Portuguese, Antonio, was allowed to stay, the Hollander,

Gaspar, was sent to Ormuz. As a compromise, however, the authority of Antonio was strictly confined to the College; the care of the missions and missionaries was confided to another.

Thus Xavier started on his voyage to Japan with a heavy heart, for he knew very well that he left behind him the seeds of serious trouble. Still, he must go. This state of things was nothing new. Whatever he had undertaken had usually come to grief; his plans had been regularly brought to naught by just those from whom he had naturally a right to expect most assistance. In two months he reached Malacca; a month later he was on his way to Japan. But not without a last sad note which betrays the anxiety he carried with him. Before he left Malacca he wrote to the Provincial of Portugal:

"As you know well, the office of superior is very dangerous for one who is not perfect. I ask you therefore to send, as rector and superior of the brethren in India, one to whom this office will do no spiritual injury. Antonio Gomez does not possess the necessary qualifications."

It was long before his request was heeded. For two years and more Xavier was away in Japan; when he returned to Goa, Gomez was still at his post. In those two years he had done serious harm; and in the meanwhile, while Francis was wearing himself out exploring Japan, he was telling his own tale to superiors in Europe. But not without the knowledge of Francis; in spite of his preoccupation far away, he found time to write to Fr. Antonio, warning him, and begging him to do his simple duty. Thus we find him saying:

"I entreat you, for the love of our Lord, so to behave that all the members of the Society may love you. Write to me and tell me of your spiritual life. If you will do that, you will lift a great burthen from my heart."

It was all of no avail. Gomez received the letters of Francis, but chose to go his own way. He claimed to have

better training than Francis; he knew better how the Indian
mission should be worked. He had the ear of his Provincial
in Portugal; Francis had not. He had the College under his
complete control expressly by the Provincial's order; Francis had other things to do. Therefore it was only just that
he should be given a free hand; he, and not Francis, had
the right to lay down the policy of the mission. Scarcely
had Francis sailed away from Goa than the native students
were dismissed in numbers; in their places were received
Portuguese youths, many of whom could scarcely read or
write. Of these many were hurried through to ordination;
this was adduced as a proof of the wisdom and success of
his policy, and Gomez then wished to close the College to
native students altogether.

Such was the news which reached Francis after a year or
more of his time in Japan. There was trouble everywhere
among the brethren in India; unless he returned it would
increase. He had no alternative but to return. In November, 1551, he set sail from Japan, and reached Malacca in
forty days. Here he received an abiding consolation, humanly speaking the greatest he had ever had during all his
time in the East, and one that buoyed him up to face the
still greater trouble to come. It was a letter from Ignatius,
the first that had reached him for four years. Its contents
had much between the lines, which even we may easily
read. We know that during this time Ignatius had had no
little trouble with Simon Rodriguez, the Provincial of Portugal, in fact with all the Portuguese Province altogether;
it was to the Province of Portugal that his famous Letter on
Obedience was written about this time. The trouble was
not unlike that between Francis and Antonio; it was chiefly
a question of jurisdiction and authority. Since Simon was
what he was, and since the spirit of Coimbra was the spirit
of Antonio, Ignatius saw the difficulties of his son Francis
in the very complaints that were made against him. There
was only one thing to do. He could not send him help, but
he could set him free. With his usual vigour of action, he
constituted India and the East a Province of its own, in-

dependent of the Province of Portugal, and appointed
Xavier its first Provincial. The letter which conveys this
message concludes with words whose full meaning only
Francis and Ignatius could have understood; but they are
characteristic, both of the saint who wrote them and of
the saint to whom they were written:

> "I shall never forget you,
> > "Entirely your own,
> > > "Ignatius."

That sentence was enough. It told again of that *interna
charitatis et amoris lex* which always ruled the heart of
Ignatius, and which he placed above all constitutions for
the government of his Society. It made up for many dis-
appointments. Before this Francis had asked for men of
better calibre than those he had received, and had been
told he could not have them. They were wanted elsewhere.
He had described the fields he had explored, white for the
harvest, and had appealed for men to whom he could trust
them; he received a scanty handful, and of these many he
had to send home again, or dismiss from the Society altogether. And we are now, be it remembered, within a year
of his death.

Francis sailed from Malacca to Cochin, and here further
trouble awaited him. During all his time in India he seems
to have had only two men on whom he could entirely rely,
Antonio Criminale, an Italian from Parma, and Gaspar
Baertz. Arrived at Cochin, he was welcomed with the news
that the former had perished, murdered by Mohammedan
raiders; and with his death again had been undone much of
Xavier's work on the Fishery Coast. Gaspar was away in
Arabia. Meanwhile the news from Goa was heart-breaking.
Antonio, the man who should have been his right hand,
and in whom he had been compelled to place all his con-
fidence, had gone from bad to worse. From being Rector
of the College he had constituted himself Vice-Provincial.
He had ignored and crushed the gentle Fr. Paul, whom
Francis had appointed to control the Society in his absence,

claiming that his credentials from Rodriguez superseded
all restrictions from Xavier. In that capacity he had given
trouble everywhere. All the native students had at last been
dismissed from the College. Down along the Fishery Coast
he had thrown everything into confusion. Customs which
Francis had wisely conceded Antonio had prohibited.
What was not done in Portugal could never be allowed
among Indian natives. In his scheme for extending colleges
he had usurped the properties of others; churches assigned
for the use of the Society he had claimed for his own. In
Goa itself the Jesuit fathers were almost in open revolt.
They no longer knew whom they were to obey.

To add to the confusion, just before the arrival of Francis
in Goa, another father had come out from Portugal, sent as
superior by Rodriguez, the Provincial. But when he presented his credentials it was noticed that they did not bear
the signature of Ignatius; evidently Rodriguez had appointed him on his own authority alone. Moreover he was
a new man, utterly unacquainted with the conditions in the
East; and the fathers had had bitter enough experience
with Antonio to risk another reformer from Portugal. He
must await the arrival of Father Francis before he could
be allowed to supersede even the dreaded existing superior.

Xavier arrived in Goa in February, 1552. He was there
only two months before he set off again on his final voyage
to China. But in those two months much had to be done.
Now that he was Provincial with power to act independ-
ently he could remove Fr. Antonio from office; at the same
time he feared to repeat his last experience with the new-
comer from Portugal. In spite of many remonstrances,
Antonio was sent to Diu, far up the coast; Francis would
listen to no entreaty, not even that of the Viceroy himself.
Still he would not instal in his place the newly-appointed
Fr. Melchior Nunez. The story is that when they met Fr.
Francis asked him: "What qualities do you possess to fit
you to be a Rector?" Fr. Melchior replied: "Six years of
theology and three of philosophy." "Would that you had six
years of experience," was Xavier's answer, and he sent him

away to Bassein to gain it. In his stead, in spite of the reasons which before had made him hesitate, he appointed Fr. Gaspar. In his hands he left everything; secretly he added this, that in the next year, when the ship set sail for Portugal, Antonio was to be dismissed and sent home with it.

On Maundy Thursday of that same year Francis set sail again, never to return. At first all seemed to go well. He was received with honour in Malacca, where he gave a friend, a certain Pereira, a letter, appointing him ambassador, to go along with him to the "King" of China. Then began more trouble. The Governor of Malacca refused to let Pereira go; he turned also on Francis, and many of his Court followed suit. Francis sailed away with another wound in his heart, accompanied by two servants, the one a Chinese, the other an Indian. "Never in all my life have I endured persecution like this, not even from pagans or Mohammedans," was his summary of his last sojourn on Portuguese soil; and in a farewell letter to Fr. Gaspar he wrote:

"Master Gaspar, you cannot imagine how I have been persecuted here in Malacca."

But even that was not all. He left Malacca in July; in November he lay a dying man on the hill-side of Sancian. The ship that had brought him had slipped away home without giving him a word of warning; there remained in the harbour a single Portuguese sloop, waiting for good weather. Xavier lay beneath a temporary shelter, open on every side, the cold north wind beating mercilessly upon him. His companions and nurses were his two boys, one a Chinese, the other an Indian; during all his illness not a single European from the vessel in the harbour went near him. So he died, deserted in death as for the most part he had been in life; within sight of a goal which again he was doomed not to reach, repeating again and again in mingled sadness and resignation: "Jesus, Son of David, have mercy on me." Meanwhile in Goa a letter from Ignatius was awaiting him, bidding him come home to Europe. He had failed in his childish ambitions, failed as a University professor, failed as a monk or a hermit, failed as an Italian preacher, failed as a Court orator, and after all that he was to reap a harvest which he was never to know. No, St. Francis Xavier, the Apostle of the East, was not wholly a success; had he been that he would have failed to resemble his Master, the Failure of Calvary. And in that very failure, more than in all his triumphs, is the real greatness of the saint to be found. For through it all he never once flinched or surrendered. He appealed to be brought home, but he did not linger for the recall. He appealed for better support, but he went on using what he had at his disposal. He saw in all his failures proof of his own incompetence; but he strove with might and main to give without reserve the little he had to give. Xavier was great, not so much because of what he did as because of what he failed to do.

This, then, is the other side of the life of one of the most successful of the chosen servants of God. There is a greater greatness than the greatness of success; and that is the greatness of failure. For that is the greatness of being, without the encouragement of doing; the greatness of sacrifice, of which others less great may reap the fruits.

What became of his beloved College of St. Paul? A visitor to Goa will find there a deserted town, with nothing standing but its churches. Palm-trees grow in the market-place, where once the grim rites of the Inquisition were performed. If he asks where stood, and what is now left of, the College of St. Paul, he will be told that the spot is out of the way and its ruins are not worth a visit. But if he insists, he will be taken a mile or so from the centre of the town towards the sea, along a road flanked by palms, and there he will find standing on his left a single wall, pierced by an arched doorway, and will almost wonder how it still stands, all alone and unsupported. It is the façade of the old church of the College; the foundations of the rest are hidden beneath a tangle of bush. If he goes a little farther, and climbs the wall that skirts the road, he will find himself in a similar waste of undergrowth. Let him work his way up through this, and he will discover still standing among the trees, the little chapel in the garden where Xavier used to hide for a month at a time from his labours, and, on the left, the well where he cooled his heart when it threatened to burst in an ecstasy of love.

The buildings of the College have gone, but the College itself still lives. Some years after the saint's death the place where the College stood became hopelessly malarial, and students and staff had to leave it. They went inland, to a more open country; and now at Rachol the great seminary of Goa preserves the tradition unbroken. It is not without significance that of all the works established by St. Francis Xavier, this, which was dearest to his heart, and cost him more than all the rest, is the only one that has survived. His spirit still broods over Southern India; there more than anywhere else may the Catholic faith be seen in all its vigour. Still, even here it would be hard to say what single area bears certain proofs of his labour. Much has been entirely swept away, by persecution and invasion; what may have survived has been merged in the work of the missionaries who have come after. Only at Rachol, the tree which he certainly planted, and watered with his heart's blood, still lives and bears the fruit for which he expressly planted it.

THE SELF-PORTRAIT OF
ST. JOHN OF THE CROSS

1542–1591

It is a curious fact that the complete life of St. John of
the Cross has never been adequately written, not even, it
would seem, in his own country. What is more, though
he has been declared a Doctor of the Church because of
his mystical writings, yet it is only of recent years that a
complete critical edition of his works has appeared. This,
at first sight, will seem all the more remarkable, since both
the life and the writings of his companion, St. Teresa, are
so well known; of her we have many excellent lives in many
languages, while her works have been edited again and
again.

But perhaps the reason is not far to seek. Though the
life of St. Teresa is one beset with many contradictions,
still even her life must yield in this respect to that of St.
John of the Cross. What makes the biographer's task more
difficult is that the contradictions arose for the most part
from good and zealous men; consequently, in order to
vindicate the saint, he is compelled to paint in darker col-
ours those whom otherwise he would prefer to honour. And
as for his writings, in spite of the sublime heights to which
in the end they reach, still there remains the apparent
severity of the hard ascetic running through them all, calling for a merciless surrender which makes the ordinary as-
pirant to a higher life despair. We acknowledge the ideal

to which he points, but we suspect it to be an ideal and nothing more; and a reader of St. John is tempted to pass by the *Ascent of Mount Carmel*, and the *Dark Night of the Soul*, for the happier pages of the *Spiritual Canticle* and the *Living Flame*.

Taken out of their context, that is, studied apart from the life and personality of their author, and apart from the circumstances in which they were written, it must be confessed that the detachment taught by St. John seems, at times, rigid and severe; while reading what he writes we almost cry out: "Who, then, shall be saved?" But there is another aspect of them which makes a great difference in our understanding, both of the author's point of view, and of the doctrine that he taught. It is that to a great extent the works of St. John were autobiographical; they were the written record of his own life, of all the hard things he had to endure, and of the lessons he had to learn from them. As he went along, so heavily did blow after blow fall upon him, that he could only keep his balance by singing to himself of the good that came out of his troubles; later, when in turn he had to teach others, he could only do it by commenting on the poem he had written in his own successive hours of trial. To interpret his works aright one needs to keep in mind all the time the author himself and his experiences; then it will be seen that what he writes is not so much an exhortation to spiritual surrender as a continual cry telling what God has taught him by means of suffering which is not easily paralleled. To illustrate this point is the object of this essay.

Juan de Yepes was the son of a poor silk weaver of Fontiberos, Toledo, and was born in 1542. His father was of noble birth; he had married much beneath him, and for that offence had been entirely cut off by his family. He had taken to silk weaving as a means of livelihood, but had never been able to make much of it. Soon after the birth of Juan he died, worn out with the effort to keep his wife and three children. The family were left in direst poverty; the children grew up always underfed, so that to the end of his life Juan remained dwarfed in stature. St. Teresa, in one of her flashes of humour, speaks of him in one place as "half a man."

Juan first went to a poor school in Medina, where the family then lived. Then he tried to learn a trade, but apparently could make nothing of it. At fourteen years of age, since he had to earn his living, he found a post as an assistant in a hospital in Medina; at the same time he contrived to attend the classes of a school conducted by the Jesuit fathers. Here at once the genius of the boy appeared. He was a born artist, and every form of art appealed to him. Music was his delight; not only the music of song and instrument, but also the "silent music," as he later called it, of the woods, and the waters, and the stars. He had a relish for sculpture; he could paint and design; but most of all he revelled in poetry, and found in it the medium for the expression of his soul. Of all things else Juan de Yepes was a poet born; with a poet's vision, a poet's ambition, a poet's restlessness and dissatisfaction, a poet's special field of delight, last of all a poet's need to find expression in rhythm and verse. We have heard much of late of the relation between poetry and mysticism; in Juan de Yepes we find the two combined, the one expressed in terms of the other, as we may perhaps find them in no other mystic, not excepting Ramon Lull.

In course of time Juan found his place among the Carmelites of Medina; he was sent by them to pursue his higher studies at the University of Salamanca. It was the heyday of that University; particularly it was the day when young Castilian poets were breaking new ground, and delighted in every manner of finesse. Juan was soon in the group; his later poetry proves it, with its mystery, its enigmatic imagery, which nevertheless he is always able to unravel; it is not unlikely that some of his well-known poems, for instance, the Canticle of Christ to the Soul, belong to those days at Salamanca. This Canticle is just a love-lyric of the period, turned to the saint's own purpose. It begins:

A little shepherd alone, in pain,
  His soul no joy can move;
His thought is all for his shepherdess,
  His heart is lost in love.

But he weeps not because of love's deep wound,
  Laments not at his lot;
Though the wound has cloven his heart in two—
  He weeps that he is forgot.

So the poet wrote his lyric, but he was not satisfied. The more he progressed, in whatever direction it might be, the more he saw ahead and hungered for it; this is the characteristic of St. John. He had become a Carmelite, it was not enough. He must give, like a poet, to the last; he must give his all. He had become a student, it was not enough. He must seek wisdom at its source, in solitude; he must become a Carthusian.

Such was Juan's state of mind, straining for the infinite, at the close of his time in Salamanca. At that moment it was that a woman came across his path; her name was Teresa. She was his elder by nearly thirty years; she too had long since learnt the lesson of solitude, and silence, and flight from the world, to gain the delights of the Interior Castle. She heard of Juan and his dreams; she met him and was satisfied. Juan, too, saw in her desires like his own. Let the world, even the world of the cloister, say what it would, he would take service with her. They would live alone, with God alone; they would think of God alone, would perceive Him alone, would love Him alone; they would die a slow death, to the world outside, to themselves, to life itself that they might lose themselves in Him only.

No sooner is the goal clear before him, than he must pursue it at all costs. This delicate little man must choose a way of life that makes even St. Teresa shiver; this sensitive man must live in a way that makes his brethren laugh; even the peasants, accustomed to hardships, could only turn up their noses at the queer thing that lived as he lived, and was content with the crusts they flung to him. The artist, the poet, the lover of all things beautiful, the noble-man within him that never died, shivered at it all as well as they, but laughed at it no less; and he went on his way victorious, for the first step had been made.

Then there came the Pharisees. Since ridicule would not deter him, prudence must intervene. Their fellow-religious had lost his head; he was a disgrace to the Institute; he was claiming to be more Catholic than the Pope himself, since he would not accept his ruling. God did not ask for exaggerations, much less would He have them flaunted as ideals; when followers began to gather round Juan, then the authorities were up in arms. He was nothing less than a conspirator, he must be suppressed and taught his place at all costs; if necessary his life must be shortened, for it was expedient that one man should die for the people that the whole nation might not perish.

So the persecution grew, and Juan, whose heart was made for love, who could sing of love as none of them all could sing of it, had to battle through it all. He was thirty-five years of age. Youth was past; manhood was ripening; an elderly woman of more than sixty was pointing out for him the way; so in surrender, amid laughter and mistrust, the search for the Holy Grail had begun.

But it was not to continue without a struggle of another kind; since scorn had not suppressed him, recourse must be had to arms. On a night in early December, 1577, Juan was seized in St. Teresa's convent, and taken home and put in prison. There he was scourged for his insubordination, given foul food and nothing to drink, and then for security spirited away to Toledo. Here for nine months he was kept, in what was little better than a hole in a wall, narrow, dark, without ventilation; fed on crusts and remnants of fish, and every Friday brought out to do penance, ending with a discipline on his naked shoulders, before the community in their refectory. Juan kept the marks of those scourgings on his body to the last day of his life.

Nor did his sufferings stop there. He was bullied by superiors, he was deprived of the sacraments; false reports were told outside his door, but carefully loud enough for him to hear, that Teresa's reform had been condemned, that the Pope himself had declared against it, that those who refused to accept the decision would be severely punished. Juan heard it all, and had no reason to believe that what he heard was not true; nevertheless within him his heart cried out that the dream he had before him came from God, that one day, if he persevered, it would be fulfilled. He fell back on his lonely prayer, and saw how all this persecution did but make it the more real; he expressed the fruit of his prayer in verse, and the result was the *Canticle* which has made his name immortal, and the poem of the *Obscure Night*, which places him at once in the front rank, both of poets and of mystics. He had lived it all, and while he had lived it he had written, not only the story of his suffering, but the meaning of that suffering in the light of the new vision that he had once dreamed and now had learnt. He had been deprived of all and the deprivation had given him everything. He had tasted all bitterness, and it had turned into sweetness. What had been difficult had become easy; what had been repugnant was now a joy; affliction was his consolation, effort his rest, the meanest and lowest things brought him new vistas of glory and of beauty. When later he taught the same to others he taught them as one who knew; not as a hardened ascetic, but as a lover of life who had discovered a new world.

This was the meaning of his Obscure Night, and of his encouragement to men to brave it. But it was not all. As he had gone deeper down into the darkness, and had seen the fruit, so he would lead others; into the night not only of all things sensible, but also of the spirit and of the soul. Again as we read him we know that he is writing from his own experience; the blackness of despair when blind faith alone can be the guide, the lack of every memory that can sustain the soul in its distress, the insipidity of every argument to steady the understanding, the bitterness, the very disgust of all things spiritual, luring the will to surrender.

He has gone through it all, and speaks of it in language that makes the sufferings of other men dwindle into insignificance; but alongside he has known no less how all this darkness leads to the glory of the sunlight. Or rather it is itself the sunlight, by the side of which the light of this world grows pale. It is not as a penance, it is as a glorious discovery, as a truth which only a poet and a seer can adequately tell, and which even he can only tell from personal experience, that Juan bids us learn all there is to learn, possess all there is to possess, know all there is to know, but to do so by a very whirlwind of annihilation of all we have and are. Give up all and gain all, the All-Beauty, the All-Light, the All-Essence, the All-Love. When we read Juan's account of those nine dark months, written by the light that filtered through a chink in the door, we understand, though it be as from a distance, that suffering, even the worst, has to a saint an aspect far different from that which the world can see.

But now opens out another phase in the making of this soul of gladness. After nine months of captivity there came an opportunity for him to escape. Should he make use of it, or should he not? To remain in the dark might teach him yet more of the glory that lay beyond it, but to go forth when occasion offered might enable him to teach his wonderful discovery to others. There was still time; worn to a skeleton as he was, there was still life and fire within him. One night, after due preparation, with the connivance, perhaps, of more than one pitying gaoler, he slipped through the corridors, he let himself down from a window by a rope made of his bed-linen, and found his way to the home of a canon in the neighbourhood, who gave him welcome and protection. Two years more, and victory for Teresa's reform was assured. The king was on her side, the Pope declared for her; in 1580 the Brief was written which made the Discalced of St. Teresa an independent province of their own. The leader now might die; within two years she went to her reward.

But all was not over for Juan; on the contrary it did but

open out a field for fresh endurance, a further struggle from which, this time, there was no escape. He had gone through two hard contests, first with those without, then with those of his Order; there remained a last surrender, that he should be rejected by those of his own household, the very followers of Teresa themselves. Teresa had gone; Juan had treasured her letters to him as only a poet can. In a moment of surrender he destroyed them, as a last sacrifice of love. If there was more yet to be given, by his own act he would show that he was prepared to give it. And his offering was accepted. Juan was at this time Prior at Granada. But now that Teresa was gone there arose a division in the ranks and she was not there to keep them together. Jealousy made its appearance, that weapon of weak souls; the strong men and women whom Teresa had held for her dearest were made the object of attack. And with jealousy came misunderstanding, or rather the determination to misunderstand; even before Teresa had died she had been compelled to stand by Juan on this account. Now she was not there to defend him. "Fervent" souls had their own ideas of the good that should be done among men; armed with prayer they must go out to others, they must preach, they must teach, they must devote themselves to the sick.

But such was not the mind of Juan, nor the mind of those who had best understood their foundress. God alone, to be sought by love alone, and by love in solitude with Him; this was the meaning of her reform, and by this means she had hoped, in her degree, to do her work for mankind. Two spirits were now at work threatening to destroy the good that had been done; and, for a time, the spirit of expansion prevailed. There was opposition, there was intrigue; by slow degrees those who held for the more interior life were removed, and Juan, the most stalwart and resolute among them, found the storm concentrated on himself. Human prudence, human ideas of utility, again rose up against him, this time allied with all that he held most dear, the brethren and sisters who, with him, claimed Teresa for their mother. For five years he fought on, almost single-handed. To preserve the teaching of the foundress intact he sacrificed his own beloved solitude. He wandered from convent to convent; he preached, he wrote, he drew up instructions, in every way he could he proved the reality of the dream of Teresa and himself. The songs of the night which he had written in Toledo were now brought out again and further explained; thus were the final works of St. John given to the world, the deepest human revelation of the mystical life.

Nevertheless he failed; and, if one who looks on from outside may say it, even till to-day the Order of Carmel has had to bear the consequence of his failure. A new régime was instituted, contrary to that which Teresa had wished; it received the sanction of the Pope, Sixtus V., and at once the storm burst. Juan at the time was Prior at Segovia, having been removed there from Granada; now began the Night of Segovia, the counterpart and the completion, in suffering and results, of the Night of Toledo. At Toledo he had learnt the complete surrender of all that nature could claim, at Segovia he learnt the surrender of his very soul; and as at Toledo he had risen to discover the glory of giving all that nature contained, so at Segovia he rose to a greater vision, the glory of utter self-annihilation in God. We can follow him from afar; we can see at a distance the beauty of the poet-saint's ideal, reached by himself though we cannot attain to it; but let us not say that, because it is beyond us, therefore his teaching is hard, and who shall hear it? "The soul that is enamoured is a tender soul, a gentle soul, a soul that is humble and patient." So wrote St. John in one of his aphorisms, and with all his stern ideals he was that from the beginning to the end.

Thus we may guess beforehand that the last ordeal would be the worst of all. This soul of purest love must be tried in a strange fire. Rome had intervened and brought peace to the distracted Order, but the Provincial who had been overruled could not and would not forgive the man who, he thought, had outwitted him. Rumours began to spread concerning Juan; whence they arose it was difficult to tell. It was said that he was a man of evil life; the report was confirmed by third-hand particulars; soon the charges were so vile, and so persistent, that Juan was asked to declare what he had to say in his defence. A canonical examination was held; some nuns were called in to bear witness; before his face they were asked questions so shameful that they refused to answer, and their silence was brought as evidence against him. For the sake of peace, so said the Provincial, he was asked to lay aside his office and go into retirement. He did as he was requested; he retired into the desert of Peñuela. But this only seemed to make matters worse. His retreat was taken as a confession; his enemies had now free scope and could say what they would; letters came to him from old friends and followers, crying shame upon him for his foulness of life and his hypocrisy.

From this time forward Juan never looked up again. For him there was no Resurrection and Forty Days. A very few still believed in him; the majority of his own brethren looked on him as something to be shunned, with whom, when one met him, it was needful to be prudent. It was even suggested that for the sake of the reputation of the Order he should leave the country. Meanwhile, alone in the desert, his health gave way beneath the burning summer sun. Fever came on; after he had endured it for more than a week he crawled back to one of the Carmelite monasteries to plead for shelter. He was given a choice between two, Baeza and Ubeda. Baeza was one of his own foundations, and his memory was still venerated in the place; at Ubeda he was known to no one except the Prior, and he had long been a pronounced enemy. The rest of the community only knew him as the man with a bad name. Juan chose Ubeda.

Here, as was to be expected, he was ill received. He had foisted himself upon the monastery; let him look to it. He was given a cell in a remote corner of the building and there deserted; not a question was asked concerning his illness or his needs. A few of the lay-brothers took pity on him; the

Prior, indignant, forbade anyone to go near him again. From time to time he visited him himself, but it was only to taunt him with old grievances, and to assure him that now he could have his revenge.

Meanwhile the malady increased. A doctor was sent for to bleed him; he was such a blunderer that once he cut the poor man to the bone. At length (it was December 13th, 1591), he said to the infirmarian, who looked in upon him: "At midnight to-night we shall be saying Matins in heaven." At once there was a transformation. The religious gathered round his bed; the Prior went down on his knees and asked his pardon. As the clock struck twelve, Juan raised his eyes, cried: "Glory be to God," and passed away. He had not completed his fiftieth year. With all this in mind let us read the writings of St. John of the Cross and we shall be struck, first, with the amount of self-disclosure they contain, second, with the beauty of the lesson which can be learnt only by suffering, above all by the suffering which comes of ignominy and shame. To-day the body of St. Teresa is preserved incorrupt, for everyone to see and honour; the body of St. John—no one knows where it lies; his very burial-place has been forgotten. Perhaps we know why; perhaps, too, we understand why to this day his life is "hidden with Christ," seeing how deeply he bore the wounds of Christ upon his body.

ST. CAMILLUS DE LELLIS
THE EX-TROOPER

1550–1614

Camillus de Lellis had a good but timid mother; his father seems to have been the very opposite. Both were of respectable, some say of noble, families; and the surname confirms it. But the father, himself the son of a fighting man, had become such a ne'er-do-weel that he had long since dragged the family name in the mud. He was a soldier all his life, or rather he was an adventurer; he served in the armies of various monarchs, hiring himself out to whoever would pay him in the manner common at that time, and was actually in the imperial army which sacked Rome in 1527. He appears to have been chiefly conspicuous for having all a soldier's vices of the period; he was a careless spendthrift and a persistent gambler. The chief consolation he gave to his wife was that he was seldom at home.

When Camillus came into the world, he brought only anxiety to his mother. He was the only child that survived his infancy; even before his birth she had a dream which she could only interpret as portending misfortune. Her husband gave her no help, and she had the burden of bringing up her boy as best she could, with a sorry example before him. As for Camillus, from the first he showed only signs of taking after his father. As a child he was lank and ungainly, unusually tall for his years, in appearance anything but attractive, lazy by nature and hating to be taught. He had a violent temper and an obstinate self-will, which were not improved by the fact that his mother feared him, and for peace's sake allowed him his own way so far as she was able. He was only twelve years of age when she died; what with her reckless husband, and what with her wayward son, who had learnt thus early to pay no heed to her, life was too much for her, and she was taken away.

For a time after her death Camillus was placed under the care of relatives, who took little interest in him; his character was not such as to win sympathy, and he was allowed to drift very much as he chose. He was sent to school, but he detested it. When he ought to have been learning he did little but dream of his father's adventures, and longed for the day when he would be grown-up enough to run away and join him; when he was out of school he found low companions for playmates, and very early became addicted to gambling. One only thing could be said for him. In spite of his waywardness he learnt from his mother a deep respect for religion. He believed in prayer, though he seldom prayed; in the sacraments, though he seldom received them; in later years we shall see how this pulled him through many a crisis, and in the end was his saving.

At length the day of liberation came. Being so tall, and having early learnt to swagger as a full-grown man, he could easily pass as being much older than he was; when he was barely seventeen he shut up his books, joined his father in a foreign camp, and enlisted as a soldier. There he allowed himself to live as he would; before he was nineteen he had learnt everything a wicked youth could learn, and made free use of his knowledge. Under his father's tuition, in particular, he became an expert gambler; from that time onward the two together, father and son, were the centre of gambling wherever they went. In fact they made gambling a profession.

There was plenty of fighting in those days, and soldiers of fortune had little difficulty in finding occupation; when their funds had run out, and idling had become a burden, Camillus and his father had only to offer their services to any general who was in need of men, and because of their previous experience they were easily accepted. Thus it was that they found themselves in all sorts of camps, sometimes fighting with friends, sometimes with enemies; an authority seems to say that at one time they were found even on the side of the Turks. Fighting to them was fighting, the cause was no affair of theirs. So long as they were paid their hire, and enjoyed the wild life they desired, the rest mattered little to them.

But this kind of existence could not go on for ever. Even among the rough soldiers of their time Camillus and his father were too great a disturbance in the camp, and once at least were turned out. Their gambling, aggravated by their own violent tempers, led to quarrels; gambling and quarrelling produced only insubordination. They took to the road, wandering from hamlet to hamlet, earning what they could by their cards. One day, as they were travelling together on foot with a view to joining the army in Venice which was being raised to fight the Turks, both of them fell ill on the road. But the father was the worse of the two; and Camillus had perforce to put up with his own sickness as best he could while he found a place where his father could be cared for. Alas! it was too late. His father's illness was too far advanced, his worn-out body had no resistance left. Camillus's only consolation was—for in spite of the life he was leading it was to him a strange and abiding consolation—that on his death-bed the old man broke down in sorrow for his past, received the last sacraments with true fervour, and died an evidently penitent man. Thus for the first time the faith he had inherited from his mother served Camillus in good stead.

Left alone in the world, and with this last scene stamped indelibly upon his memory, Camillus began to reflect. He was reduced by his gambling habit to utter destitution of both body and soul; death might overtake him at any time, as it had overtaken his father, and there might be no one to help him in his need. He would mend his ways; he would escape from all further temptation by hiding himself in a monastery, if a monastery could be induced to accept him; there and then he took a vow to become a Franciscan. He remembered that he had a Franciscan uncle somewhere in Aquila; he would begin with him. As soon as he was well enough he tramped off, came to his uncle's door, told him his tale, and asked that he might be admitted into the Order. His uncle received him kindly and listened to his story, but was not easily convinced. Vocations did not come so easily as that; Camillus would need further trial that his constancy might be proved. Besides, at the moment he was in no fit state to enter on religious life. Not only was he worn in body, but he had a running wound above his ankle, which had started long ago with a mere nothing, but had obstinately refused to be healed. The Franciscans were kind, but they could not think of receiving Camillus as a postulant, and he was once more sent adrift.

And he did drift; first to old boon companions, with whom he took up again his gambling habits; then, since the running sore in his leg became a nuisance to others, he began to wander alone from place to place, scarcely knowing how he lived. It was indeed a long and trying probation for one who was to become the apostle of the derelict and dying. At length he found his way to Rome; and here the thought occurred to him that if he could gain admission to some hospital the wound in his leg might be tended and cured. He applied at the hospital of S. Giacomo; as he had no money with which to pay for a bed, he offered himself as a servant in the place, asking in return that his running sore might be treated. It is well to remember that at this time, since the Franciscans had rejected him, his chief ambition was to be cured that he might once more return to the life of a soldier.

On the conditions he proposed he was received and given a trial. At first all seemed to go well. Camillus was in earnest, and meant to do his best; away from his old surroundings the better side of Camillus appeared. He went about his work with a will, sweeping corridors, cleaning bandages, performing all the most menial duties of the place, for he was fit for nothing else. The doctors on their part did theirs, attending to his wound, and giving him hope of a permanent cure; under this régime one might have trusted that a change had come in his life at last. But unfortunately for him, in spite of the work allotted to him, he had many idle hours on his hands; and there were never wanting other idle servants about him with whom he was able to spend them. In spite of all his good intentions his old passion for gambling returned and he could not resist. He secured a pack of cards, and to wile away the time he taught his games to his companions. But soon the authorities began to notice that something was going wrong in the servants' quarters. The men were less ready at their work; they were dissatisfied among themselves; quarrelling became more common, for with the return of the gambling habit Camillus's ill-temper returned in its wake. A search was made of his room; the telltale cards were found hidden in Camillus's bed. Without more ado he was pushed into the street, his leg still unhealed, and without a coin in his pocket.

So for a second time Camillus's efforts to mend his ways came to nothing. He became despondent; his evil habits had the better of him and he seemed unable to control them; he would go back to soldiering again and take his chance. Hence the next we hear of him is once more in the armies of Venice; he fought in those ranks against the Turks, while he was still only nineteen years of age. He continued there for two years, fighting by land and sea. Still even here his evil genius pursued him. He distinguished himself, it is said, on the battle-field, but in camp once more got himself into trouble. On one occasion, at Zara, a gambling quarrel led to a challenge; a duel was arranged between himself and another soldier, and only the interference of the sergeant of his company prevented it. In the end, good enough soldier as he was, his seniors seem to have grown tired of him and he was dismissed.

But dismissal did not cool Camillus's fighting spirit. Since Venice would not have him any longer, he went and

joined the army of Spain. Later on, in 1574, he is found
in a company of adventurers, under one Fabio; its chief attraction for Camillus was that every man in it was addicted
to gambling. In this company he fought in North Africa
and elsewhere; at last, on their way to Naples from
Palermo, their galleys were so tossed about by a storm that
they were given up for lost, and they finally landed with
nothing but the clothes on their backs and their weapons of
war. The company had to be disbanded, and once again
Camillus was a homeless tramp. He went straight to the
gambling dens which he knew well. There he staked all he
had—his sword, his gun, his powder flasks, his soldier's coat,
and he lost them all; he was thankful that at least he had
his shirt on his back, for even that, on a former occasion
in that same place, he had staked and lost, and had been
forced to part with in public.

He now sank lower than ever; what was worse, he found a
companion in his misery. The two formed a sort of partnership. Gambling from town to town became their trade,
with begging to make up when they had lost everything.
Worst of all, Camillus in a kind of hopeless despair seemed
to have no will left; he went wherever and did whatever
his evil comrade directed him to go and to do. They had a
vague idea that they would travel about and see the world;
if fighting came their way, they would join up again as
they had done before; this was Camillus's condition in
1574, when he was twenty-four years of age. Just then, if
one had searched all the dens of Italy, it might have been
difficult to find a more hopeless case than that of Camillus
de Lellis.

And yet just then the change came. The two tramps had
come to Manfredonia. One morning they were begging,
with others of their kind, standing on the steps outside a
church. It chanced that among the passers-by was a man
of wealth, well known for his charitable works. He noticed
the tall, soldier-like youth among the beggars. He spoke to
him, expressed his surprise that one such as he should be
begging his bread among cripples and other helpless crea-

tures, and told him that he ought to work. Camillus made the usual excuses; he said that he was a disbanded soldier and that now no one would employ him. The rich man took him at his word. At the time he was building a monastery outside the town; he gave Camillus no money, but sent him with a note of instruction that he should be given employment on the building.

Camillus accepted the offer, and made up his mind to try; but first he must take leave of his old companion and dissolve their partnership. His comrade, when he heard his announcement, could not but burst into laughter at this sudden conversion. He mocked at Camillus, so quickly turned pious; he showed him the liberty he was throwing away. He sneered at the idea that Camillus would ever persevere; he warned him that the old craving would come back again and he would give way. He would gamble with the other workmen, many of whom would not need to be taught; he would quarrel as he had done before; he would again be dismissed, and would be left more destitute than ever. Besides, the work offered him was only a trap. Under such management he would be watched everywhere; he would be always under restraint; he might as well go to prison. How much better would it be for them both to get out of Manfredonia and look for work elsewhere! Then they could do as much or as little as they liked, and when they were tired of it could go out once more on the road.

At first Camillus listened to his tempter and yielded. It was true he could not trust himself; it was also true that he could not easily surrender the free life he had been living. He turned aside, and went down the street with his companion, following him blindly as he had done before. They left Manfredonia and made for the next town, more than twelve miles away. But on the road there came to Camillus a great grace. He had felt the goodwill of the man who had offered him work; thought of the Franciscan monastery brought back to him memories of his early efforts to amend, five or six years before; it seemed to him that here was an opportunity which should not be missed, and which might never occur again. With a mighty effort, the greatest he ever made in all his life, he shook himself free. To the surprise of his companion he suddenly turned round, and began to run back to Manfredonia as fast as his legs would carry him. Next morning he found himself enrolled among the labourers on the monastery building.

Still it was no easy task. As might have been expected from one with a past like that of Camillus, he found hard work anything but a trifle. He hated the drudgery; moreover there came upon him the consciousness that he was born for something better. There followed dreams of the life he had lived. With all its squalor and misery at least it had been free; however low he had sunk he had not starved; and there had come occasions when he had had a good time. Then his old companion discovered his whereabouts, and would come around the place. He would taunt Camillus with his slave's life, would contrast his own freedom as he went to and fro at his pleasure, would provoke in him the temptation to gamble which Camillus could scarcely resist. And last there was the wound in his leg. The more he laboured the worse it troubled him; the particular task that was assigned to him only tended to aggravate the pain.

Nevertheless Camillus laboured on. The skilled work of the builder was beyond him, but there were other employments to keep him always occupied. He drove the donkeys that carried the stones for the building in panniers on their backs; he took the messages into the town; he brought the other labourers their food and drink. Curious neighbours could not but observe this tall youth in rags with that about him which showed that he had seen better days, but he took no heed. The only remaining sign of his former life was the soldier's belt he still wore; the children in the street were quick to notice this and made fun of the trooper turned donkey-driver. Camillus was stung by these trifles; he could endure many things, but could not endure to be ridiculed. Still he held on; whatever happened he must keep to his post; that was almost all his ambition for the present, and his many past failures had taught him where he must be on his guard if he would succeed. If he would check his gambling propensity he must keep to himself and away from danger; if he would conquer his habit of idle dreaming he must be always occupied; if he would subdue his temper he must submit to whatever was put upon him; if he would suppress the multitudinous temptations that surged within him, he must make himself work and work. He could look back afterwards and recognise that those months spent as a driver of donkeys were the turning-point of his life.

It was a humble beginning, solitary, drab, without sensation of any kind; it had not even the dramatic climax of a sudden great conversion like that of Augustine and others. Nevertheless it was the beginning of a saint. Camillus worked on, and soon two things followed. He began to have more confidence in himself, and he began to win the good opinion of others; with the first came an aspiration to rise to better things, with the latter the means to attain them. We are explicitly told that when first he undertook the work at the building his only ambition was to get through the winter, and to earn a few crowns with which to start life again in the spring; after all, even that was something when we consider what he had been immediately before. But he had no intention, and even feared, to go further. When some Capuchins, for whom the monastery was being built, offered him some of their cloth to replace his rags he refused it; he was afraid lest to accept it might lead to other things, perhaps to his becoming a friar. But before the winter was over all this had changed. One day, as he was driving his donkeys back from the town, he received the reward of his perseverance. He seemed to see himself, and all the life he had hitherto lived, in an entirely new light. The memory of the vow he had made long ago came back to him, and he began to ask himself whether his present occupation was not an opportunity given to him to fulfil it. The thought sank deeper; he remembered how once he had hoped that this might be an escape from his miserable life. He spoke of it to one of the friars, and he was encouraged. Encouragement revived desire, and soon he was at the superior's feet, asking that he might be received.

In this way Camillus gained admission into a Franciscan monastery. But his stay did not last long. No sooner had he begun his noviciate than the wound above his ankle began to grow worse. He was told that he must go; with this impediment upon him he could not be received; but for his consolation he was given the assurance that so soon as ever his running sore was healed he would be taken back. Armed with this promise Camillus set to work in earnest; he would begin again where he had begun before and failed, but he would not fail again. He would go to Rome, to the hospital of S. Giacomo, where he had received so much benefit before both for body and for soul, but from which he had been so ignominiously, and so deservedly, expelled. He would ask to be given another chance, to be taken in on the same terms as formerly. For almost a year he had kept away from gambling; he had learnt to work as he had never worked in all his life; the Franciscan fathers would give him a good character; he himself would let the authorities see that they might trust him; perhaps they would let him try again.

Camillus came to Rome, and all seemed to go well; it was in 1575, a holy year. He was given another trial at S. Giacomo, and this time there were no complaints. Camillus had heard of St. Philip Neri, of his wonderful power in supporting sinners; he made himself known to him, and St. Philip took him in charge. Under his wise guidance Camillus kept steady; he worked at the hospital for four years as a menial servant, after which it appeared that the wound in his leg was healed. Then once more he wished to return to the Capuchins. St. Philip tried to dissuade him, but he would not listen. He had made a vow; the Capuchins had promised that when his leg was healed they would have him back and he would go. But scarcely had he entered than the trouble began again; the wound broke out afresh and he was told to depart, this time with the emphatic injunction that he must not hope to try any more. Thus for the third occasion Camillus's ambition to become a friar was frustrated. He tried again the next year, with the Observantines of Ara Coeli, and was again refused; only then did he give up all hope altogether.

"God bless you, Camillus," was St. Philip Neri's welcome when he returned, "did I not tell you?"

Camillus was thirty years of age when he made his Franciscan experiment. For the last five years he had served faithfully at S. Giacomo; therefore, when he had failed at the monastery he was gladly taken back. More than that, he was appointed superintendent of the servants, and that in those days included the nurses, who were all men. Now it was that the real Camillus began to appear. Whether it was his Franciscan experience which had given him new ideals, or whether it was St. Philip who was training him to better things, from this moment Camillus became a new man. He had already learnt the value of unceasing work as a cure for his many temptations; now he discovered that the more he gave himself to helping others the happier man he became. He began to love the patients in the hospital, not merely to serve them; and the more he loved them the more he was troubled by the treatment they received, even in so comparatively well-regulated a hospital as S. Giacomo. One evening, as he stood in the middle of a ward, the thought occurred to him that good nursing depended on love; that the more it was independent of mere wages the better it would be; that if he could gather men about him who would nurse for love, and would leave the wages to look after themselves, then he might hope to raise nursing to the standard he desired.

With this object in his mind Camillus carefully selected five men from among his fellow-servants in the hospital. He told them of his ideal, and of the way he hoped to attain it; the men rose to his suggestion, and agreed to throw in their lot with Camillus, pooling all their earnings, and living as much as possible together. But soon it was

found this did not work; living in a public hospital, part of
a general staff, they could not keep separate from the rest.
If they wished to carry out their intention to the full they
must have a home of their own.

Meanwhile another thought had come to Camillus. He
had noticed that not only the servants often failed in their
duty to the sick, but the priests failed as well; if he would
have his company of nurses equal to his ambition, then
it must include priests also. He would become one himself; illiterate as he was he set to work. First he found a
chaplain of the hospital who undertook to teach him Latin
during his leisure hours; later, since by this means he made
slow progress, he entered himself as a student at the Roman College, taught by the Jesuit fathers; and, at the age
of thirty-two this lank figure of over six feet was henceforth to be seen among the little boys learning the elements
of grammar. Naturally the boys were amused; they nick-
named Camillus the "Late Arrival," and would offer him
their services to help him in his lessons. But Camillus
persevered, and in 1584, when he was thirty-four years of
age, he had the consolation of being ordained.

Now at last it may be said that the life of Camillus really
began. He took a house by the Tiber, in the lowest and
most pestilential part of the city, and there set about the
service of the sick wherever he might find them. One in-
cident here is worthy of mention; it is said to be the only
occasion when St. Philip Neri made a mistake in the
diagnosis of anyone entrusted to his spiritual care. So long
as Camillus was safe at his work in the hospital of S.
Giacomo, St. Philip was happy about him; when he heard
that he had left the place, and had taken up his abode in
the lowest quarters of the town, he was not a little dis-
tressed. Knowing Camillus's past, and his propensity
for gambling, he was much afraid that his new surroundings would only revive the old temptation. Moreover he
was convinced that this new departure was only another
mark of that restless and obstinate nature which had already made his penitent seek in vain for admission among

the Franciscans. He spoke sharply to Camillus; he advised
him, for his own security, not to give up the work he was
doing at S. Giacomo; if he disobeyed, Philip would be compelled to give him up. But Camillus held firm to his proj-
ect; he knew he had found his true vocation and he would
not yield, even though he loved St. Philip as more than a
father; and from that moment, for a period at least, Philip
Neri and Camillus de Lellis parted company. It is one
more instance of the difference that can come even between the most charitable, and the most understanding,
of saints.

It is not our object to speak of the wonderful Order, the
Brothers of a Happy Death, which grew out of these humble beginnings; it is more to our purpose to watch how
the mind of Camillus himself seemed steadily to expand,
and how to each new light he responded without any reserve. At first he had the idea of founding an institution
of hospital nurses; soon he realised that the sick outside
hospitals were in far more need of good nursing than those
within, and at once he made them the object of his special
care. Next, in a time of pestilence, he saw how the stricken
were, almost of necessity, neglected and allowed to die as
they might; he bound himself and his followers by vow to
visit pestilential areas whenever there was need, and in fulfilment of that vow numbers of his disciples gave their
lives. Following on this was his care of those actually dying. When the end was certain, many, especially among the
poor, were left to their fate and nothing more was done
for them; Camillus made the comfort and help of the dying so much his special object of charity that from that
work alone his Order ultimately took its name.

So did his charity expand, and the memory of his own
early days spurred him on, some would say, even to extravagance. No case was too abandoned for him to help;
none too wicked for Camillus to put it away. Once, in
1590, in a time of famine and distress in the city, when,
besides, the winter was exceptionally severe, Camillus was
distributing clothes to the poor in his courtyard. Two of

the recipients, as soon as they had the clothes in their hands, immediately gambled them away or sold them, and then ran off lest Camillus might discover what they had done. But Camillus was too quick for them; his old days told him why they had run away, and he sympathised. He followed after them and caught them up; then he brought them back and clothed them again as if nothing had happened. Naturally his friends remonstrated. They thought Camillus had not noticed what the rascals had done, and told him, bidding him leave them to their fate. But Camillus did not change.

"What, my brothers," he replied, "do you see nothing but the rags of these poor creatures? And do you see nothing beneath the rags but the poor creatures themselves? St. Gregory gave to a man in rags, but the man was Jesus Christ Himself."

This story is only one of many. Of all the great apostles of charity perhaps there is none of whom so many stories are told of extreme generosity to the poorest of the poor. And we in modern times have reason to preserve the memory of Camillus, for we owe him two great debts. In the first place he may be said to be the founder of the modern nursing spirit; in the second place, without any doubt, we are indebted to him for the institution of the Red Cross. When the Order which he founded was formally approved by the Pope, that its members might be distinguished from other regulars, Camillus asked that they might be permitted to wear a red cross on their cassock and mantle. By an apostolic brief, dated 26th June, 1586, the permission was granted; and three days later, on the Feast of Ss. Peter and Paul, Camillus with a few of his followers came to St. Peter's, each wearing the red cross, and there dedicated themselves and their work to God for all time.

But the charity of Camillus was not confined only to the sick and dying; it spread out to every phase of wretched humanity, no matter where he found it. As he grew older he seemed to recall with greater vividness the miseries of his early days; often enough, when his companions or others ventured to protest against what seemed to them excess, he would only answer that he himself had once been in the same or greater need, and would go on as before. When he travelled, he invariably filled his purse with small coins, to be given to beggars on the way; sometimes, for the same purpose, he would have bags of bread tied to his saddle. He would imitate literally the Samaritan in the Gospel; if he found a sufferer on the road, he would take him to the nearest inn, have him cared for, and leave behind money for his maintenance while he stayed. Indeed, this constant habit of paying for the needs of others whom he met anywhere, and who seemed in any way poorer than himself, was often a source of no small embarrassment to those who travelled with him. Camillus never seemed to care; he was always giving; when his stock ran out he would keep an account of the needs of others and would send them shoes, and clothes, and the like as soon as he was able. Not even the poverty of his own house would stop him; once when a father-prefect had forbidden the distribution of bread at the gate, because there was not enough for the community, Camillus bade him revoke his order.

"Did you sow and reap this bread?" he asked him. "I tell you, that if you will not do good to the poor, God will not do good to you; in the hour of your death it shall be measured out to you with the same measure with which you have measured out to such as these."

And again, when his disciples were afraid of his seemingly reckless giving, he said to them:

"Trust in God, O cowards, and cast your bread into the river of life; soon you shall find it in the ocean of eternity."

Or when at least they suggested that it was enough to help those who came to them, he said:

"If no poor could be found in the world, men ought to go in search of them, and dig them up from underground to do them good, and to be merciful to them."

Indeed, if one may distinguish the charity of Camillus from that of any hero of his class it was specially this: he was for ever "digging out the poor from underground to do them good." No one knew the slums or the ghetto of Rome better than Camillus; and all whom he found there, Christians or Jews or Turks, were all the same to him. He frequented the prisons; he would shave and wash the wretched convicts, and bade his companions do the same; he had special care of those condemned to death. Even the undiscovered poor did not escape him; he would inquire from neighbours whether they knew of widows or children in straitened circumstances, and when he found them, those widows and children would find parcels of money and clothes coming to them from they knew not where.

Lastly we must mention his care of the very animals. He once found a newborn lamb lying in a ditch, apparently forgotten by the shepherds. He got off his horse, picked up the lamb and carried it in his cloak to the nearest sheep-fold, where he gave it to those who would look after it. Another time he came across a dog with a broken leg. He cared for it and fed it regularly; when he had to leave the place he asked others to continue to look after it.

"I, too, have had a bad leg," he said; "and I know the misery of not being able to walk. This is a creature of God, and a faithful creature, too. If I am as faithful to my master as a dog is to his, I shall do very well."

As we read incidents and sayings like these we seem to see the secret of the sanctity of Camillus; a depth of human sympathy, and virility, and love of life itself, which was at once the cause of his early wanderings and of his later heroism. In all greatness there is a certain disregard of consequences, be it in good or in evil; we say that the greatest mountains cast the deepest shadows. So was it with Camillus. In his early years this disregard led him to choose the life he did; later it would almost seem that it left him without any power to choose for himself at all. But one day, on a sudden, he seemed to awake. He saw something he had not seen before; he felt within himself a power to be and do which was not his own. Up to that time he had often tried and failed; from that moment he failed no more. He made many mistakes; for years he was compelled to grope about; feeling his way, not knowing where he would end, perhaps not altogether caring. Still, during those years of groping it is clear that his will-power was being strengthened every day. It is not a little significant that whereas at the age of twenty-three he had not the will to resist a fellow-tramp, when he was thirty he could hold his own conviction against even a St. Philip Neri.

Once this will-power had been gained the rest of the growth of Camillus is comparatively easy to explain. He was a soldier by profession, for whom life had no surprises, to whom no degree of degradation came as a shock; he had gone through the worst and he knew. But he also knew that however low a man may fall he remains still a man; when he himself had been at his lowest he had never quite lost the memory of better things, nor the vague desire that he might be other than he was. From his own experience he was sure that the most wretched of men was more to be pitied than to be condemned; and if to be pitied, then to be helped if that was possible. With this knowledge, burnt into his soul during ten bitter years, and with the will now developed to act, the hero latent in Camillus began to appear. Nothing could stop him; not the anxious warning of a saint, not the discouragement of religious superiors, not the appeals of seculars who bade him be content with the good he was doing, not his own want of education, which seemed to exclude all possibility of the priesthood, not his naturally passionate nature, signs of which are manifest in him to the end. Like other saints, he began with nothing; as with them, the bread he gave multiplied within his hands; even more than has been the case with most saints, the stream he has set flowing has not been confined within the limits of a religious Order, but has overflowed its banks, and has materially affected the whole of our civilization.

Such has been the working of the grace of God in and

through Camillus de Lellis, the trooper, the tramp. He founded his Congregation, and it was approved, in 1586, when he was thirty-six years of age. It was raised to the rank of an Order in 1591, and Camillus was appointed its first General. He held that office till 1607, when he persuaded his brethren, and the ecclesiastical authorities, to allow him to resign. He lived for seven years more, a humble subject in the Order which he himself had founded; and, as is not uncommon in the lives of saints, if we may judge from certain signs, they were not the happiest years of his life. In 1613 it became evident to himself and to his brethren that he could not live much longer, and at his own request he was taken to Rome, that he might die in the Holy City. But his preparation for death was characteristic of his life; so long as he could drag himself about he could not be kept from visiting the hospitals. When he could no longer go out, he still continued to visit the sick in his own house; and when that became impossible, then he set himself to writing many letters, to the many in the world who had helped him with their alms, and to his own brethren, that they might continue the good work. For himself, he did not forget what he had been.

"I beseech you on my knees to pray for me," he said to the General of the Carmelites, who visited him on his death-bed, "for I have been a great sinner, a gambler, and a man of bad life."

As his mind began to wander it always went in the direction of God's mercy; he seemed never to tire of thanking Him for all He had done, through the merits of the Precious Blood of Christ. At length the end came. He stretched out his arms in the form of a cross, pronounced again his thanksgiving for the Blood of Christ, and died. It was in the evening of July 14th, 1614.

ST. JOSEPH OF CUPERTINO
THE DUNCE

1603–1663

If ever a tiny child began life with nothing in his favour it was Joseph of Cupertino; he had only one hopeful and saving quality—that he knew it. Other boys of his own age were clever, he was easily the dullest of them all. Others were winning and attractive, nobody ever wanted him. While they had pleasant things said to them, and nice things given to them, Joseph always wrote himself down an ass, and never looked for any special treatment. He went to school with the rest of the children in the village, but he did not succeed in anything. He was absent-minded, he was awkward, he was nervous; a sudden noise, such as the ringing of a church-bell, would make him drop his school-books on the floor. He would sit with his companions after school-hours, and try to talk like them, but every time his conversation would break down; he could not tell a story to the end, no matter how he tried. His very sentences would stop in the middle because he could not find the right words. Altogether, even for those who pitied him, and wished to be kind to him, Joseph was something of a trial.

Ill fortune seemed to have set its seal on Joseph before he was born. His father, a carpenter by trade, was a good enough man in his way, but he was a poor hand at dealing with money; what little he earned seemed to slip at once through his fingers. At the very moment when his son came into the world his house was in the hands of bailiffs, and his effects were being sold up. Joseph was born in a shed at the back of the house, where his mother had hid herself out of very shame. With such a beginning Joseph had very poor prospects. As a child, utterly underfed and sickly, he was a very miserable specimen of humanity. He seemed to catch every disease that came his way; many a time he was at death's door, and, to tell the truth, if he had died it would have been a great relief to those responsible for him. Even his mother wearied of him. She, too, was good in her way, but she was hard by nature, and circumstances had made her harder; Joseph was ever in fault, and for every offence she punished him without mercy, according to her notions of a mother's duty. When he was little more than seven years old he developed a running ulcer which would not heal; and his mother was the more embittered against him, for now she supposed that even if the boy grew up he would probably be always to the family nothing but a burden.

Nobody wanted Joseph; even his mother did not want him; Joseph learnt this lesson very early and accepted it. He did not seem to want himself, he did not know what he wanted; at times he seemed scarcely to know what he was doing. So abstracted was he that he would forget his meals; and when his attention was called to the fact his only reply would be: "I forgot." Since he could make nothing of books, he was apprenticed to a shoemaker. It was of little use; Joseph was too much distracted, too much absorbed in other things not practical for work-a-day people; and he never learnt to make or mend a shoe. But he went on trying and his master tolerated him, merely to give the boy something to do.

At length, one day, in the midst of this aimless life, when Joseph was already seventeen years of age, there came into his village a begging friar. At once a new idea came into Joseph's mind. He could not be anything in the world, because he seemed incapable of learning anything; strangely enough this thought had never troubled him much. But surely he could at least be a friar, and go about begging his bread. Brains were not needed for such a life as that; and as for the life itself, it appealed to him with a strange fascination, as having an ideal of its own. Besides he had two uncles in the Order; that gave him hope and encouragement.

He was easily given leave to go away from his home and try; but to find entrance into a monastery was by no means so easy. He had done no studies worth the name, and therefore could not be received; many other reasons were easily forthcoming. He applied at one convent; and the door was closed to him at once; at another, and was told it was quite hopeless; at length he found a community which agreed to take him on trial as a lay-brother. But it was of no avail; with the best of intentions to be kind to him, the brethren found him a test of their patience. Not only was he very dull and difficult to teach, but his fits of piety and abstraction, which had been with him from the beginning, made him quite unbearable. He had a way of suddenly standing still in the midst of some occupation, and forgetting everything. He would go down on his knees in the most unlikely places, utterly oblivious of everything around him. He might be washing dishes in the scullery, he might be carrying food into the refectory; one of these fits of abstraction would come on, and down everything would crash in pieces on the floor. In the hope of curing him, bits of the broken plates were fastened to his habit, and he carried them about, as a penance, as a humiliation, as a reminder not to do the same again, but he did not mend. He could not even be trusted with serving out the bread, for the reason that he forgot the difference between brown bread and white.

It was of no use. Materially or spiritually Joseph's stay in the monastery could serve no good purpose; his habit was taken from him and he was told to go. That day, as he afterwards declared, was the hardest day in all his life; it looked as if everything in heaven and earth had conspired to shut him out; and he never forgot it. He used to

say that when they deprived him of the habit it was as if
they had torn off his skin. But that was not the end of his
troubles. When he had recovered from his stupor on the
road outside he found he had lost some of his lay clothes.
He was without a hat; he had no boots or stockings, his
coat was moth-eaten and worn. Such a sorry sight did he
appear, that as he passed a stable down the lane some dogs
rushed out on him, and tore what remained of his rags to
still worse tatters.

Having escaped from the dogs, poor Joseph trudged
along, wondering what next would happen. He passed some
shepherds tending sheep. They took him for a dangerous
character. When questioned he could give no account of
himself and they were about to give him a beating; for-
tunately one of them had a little pity, and persuaded them
to let him go free. But it was only to pass from one trouble
into another. Scarcely had he gone a little further down
the road when a nobleman on horseback met him. The
latter could see in Joseph nothing but a suspicious tramp
who had no business in those parts, and thought to hand
him over to the police; only when, after examining him,
he had come to the conclusion that he was too stupid to
be harmful did he let him go.

At last, torn and battered and hungry, Joseph came to
a village where one of his uncles lived. He was a prosperous
tradesman there, with a thriving little shop of his own;
and Joseph hoped he would find with him some kind of
comfort, perhaps another start in life. But he was sadly
disappointed. Nephews of Joseph's type, even at their best,
are not always welcome to prosperous uncles, much less
when they turn up unexpectedly, with scarcely a rag on
their backs. Joseph's uncle was no better and no worse than
others. He looked at the poor lad who stood before him,
soiling his clean shop floor with his dirty, bare feet, dis-
gracing himself and his house with his rags, and he was
just a little ashamed to own him as a nephew. Evidently,
he said to himself, the boy had inherited his father's im-
provident ways, and would come to nothing good. He was

already well on the road to ruin; to help him would only
make him worse. Besides, Joseph's father already owed him
money; how, then, could he be expected to do anything
for the son?

So instead of offering him assistance, Joseph's uncle
turned upon him; blamed him for his sorry plight, which,
he said, he must have brought upon himself; railed at him
because of his father's debts, which such a son could only
increase; finally pushed him into the street, without a coin
to help him on his way. There was nothing to be done; he
must move on; nobody wanted Joseph.

At last he reached his native town, and made for his
mother's cottage. His father was still in difficulties; during
Joseph's absence things had gone no better than before.
He came to the door in fear and trembling, remembering
well how both his father and his mother had long since
tired of his presence. Still he would venture; it was the
only place left where he might hope for a shelter and he
must try. He opened the door and looked in; inside he
found his mother, busy about her little hovel. Weary and
footsore, hungry and miserable, no longer able to stand, he
fell on the floor at his mother's feet; he could not speak
a word, though his glistening eyes as he looked up at her
were eloquent.

But they failed to soften his mother. She had gone
through hard times enough and was unprepared for more.
What? Had he come back to burden them, now when
things were worse than ever? And further disgraced, besides, for had he not been expelled from a monastery? How
the neighbours would talk, and scorn the mother for having
such a son; an unfrocked friar, a ne'er-do-weel, a common
tramp, and that at an age when other youths were earning
an honest livelihood! She could restrain herself no longer.
As he lay at her feet she rounded on him.

"You have been expelled from a house of religious," she
cried. "You have brought shame upon us all. You are good
for nothing. We have nothing for you here. Go away; go

to prison, go to sea, go anywhere; if you stay here there is
nothing for you but to starve."

But she was not content with only words. She had a
brother who was a Franciscan, holding some sort of office.
In high dudgeon she went off to him, and gave him a piece
of her mind about the way his Order had dismissed her
son, and put him again on her hands. She appealed to him
to have him taken back, in any capacity they liked; so long
as she was rid of him, they could do with him what they
chose. But as for readmission, the good Franciscans were
immovable. Joseph had been examined before, and had
been declared unsuitable; he had been tried, and had been
found wanting; the most they could do was to give him
the habit of the Third Order, and employ him somewhere
as a servant. He was appointed to the stable; there he could
do little harm. Joseph was made the keeper of the monastery mule.

And then the change came. Joseph set about his task;
since it was now clear that he could never be a Franciscan,
at least he could be their servant. He said not a word in
complaint; what had he to complain of? He told himself
that all this was only what he might have expected; being
what he was, he might consider himself fortunate to find
any job at all entrusted to him. He asked for no relief; he
took the clothes and the food they chose to give him; he
slept on a plank in the stable, it was good enough for him.
What was more, in spite of his dullness, perhaps because
of it, Joseph had by nature a merry heart. However great
his troubles, the moment a gleam of sunshine shone upon
him he would be merry and laugh. The troubles were only
his desert and were to be expected; when brighter times
came he enjoyed them as one who had received a consolation wholly unlooked for, and wholly undeserved.

Gradually this became noticed. Friars would go down
to the stable for one reason or another, and always Joseph
was there to welcome them, apparently as happy as a lord.
It was seen how little he thought of himself, how glad he
was to serve; since he could not be a begging friar, some-

times in his free moments he went out and begged for them on his own account. His lightheartedness was contagious; his kindly tongue made men trust him; it was noticed how he was welcomed among the poorest of the poor, who saw better than others the man behind all his oddities. He might make a Franciscan after all. The matter was discussed in the community chapter; his case was sent up to a provincial council for favourable consideration; it was decided, not without some qualms, to give him yet another trial.

In this way Joseph was once more admitted to the Order, but what was to be done with him then? His superiors set him to his studies, in the hope that he might learn enough to be ordained, but the effort seemed hopeless. With all his good intentions he learnt to read with the greatest difficulty, and, says his biographer, his writing was worse. He could never expound a Sunday Gospel in a way to satisfy his professors; one only text seemed to take hold of him, and on that he could always be eloquent; speaking from knowledge which was not found in books. It was a text of St. Luke (xi, 27): *Beatus venter qui te portavit*. Nevertheless he succeeded in being ordained, and the story of his success is one of those mysteries of grace, repeated in the lives of other saints, down to that of the Curé d'Ars in the last century, by which Christ Himself lets us see that for His priesthood He chooses "whom He will Himself," no matter what regulations man may make.

It came about in this way. Minor Orders in those days were easily conferred, and even the subdiaconate; but for the diaconate and the priesthood a special examination had to be passed, in presence of the bishop himself. As a matter of form, but with no hope of success, Joseph was sent up to meet his fate. The bishop opened the New Testament at haphazard; his eye fell upon the text *Beatus venter qui te portavit*, and he asked Joseph to discourse upon it. To the surprise of everyone present Joseph began, and it seemed as if he would never end; he might have been a Master in Theology lost in a favourite theme. There could

be no question about his being given the diaconate. A year
later came the priesthood, and Joseph had again his ordeal
to undergo. He was examined with a number of others.
One by one the first candidates were tested, and their an-
swers were far above the average. At length the bishop,
more than satisfied with what he had heard, cut the examination short, and passed the rest unquestioned. Joseph
was among the fortunate candidates who were asked nothing, and was ordained along with the rest. He was twenty-
five years of age.

There were many, by this time, besides the very poor
who had come to realise the wonderful simplicity and self-
lessness of Joseph, hidden beneath his dullness and odd
ways; a few had discovered the secret of his abstractedness,
when he would lose himself in the labyrinth of God.
Nevertheless he remained a trial, especially to the practi-
cal-minded; to the end of his life he had to endure from
them many a scolding. Often enough he would go out begging for the brethren, and would come home with his sack
full, but without a sandal, or his girdle, or his rosary, or
sometimes parts of his habit. His friends among the poor
had taken them for keepsakes, and Joseph had been utterly
unaware that they had gone. He was told that the convent
could not afford to give him new clothes every day. "Oh!
Father," was his answer, "then don't let me go out any
more; never let me go out any more. Leave me alone in
my cell to vegetate; it is all I can do."

For indeed, as we have seen, Joseph had no delusions
about himself; and his ordination did not make him think
differently. He had been sorely knocked about in life, but
he always understood that he deserved it. The poor in the
villages, when he went among them to beg, showed him
peculiar respect and friendship; but he always took this to
mean that they looked on him as one of themselves, indeed rather less than they were, and they were kind to him
out of pity. True he was a priest, but everybody knew how
he had received the priesthood. He could assume no airs
on that account. On the contrary, knowing what he was,

he could only act accordingly. In spite of his priestly office, Joseph could only live the life he had lived before. He would slip down to the kitchen and wash up the dishes; he would sweep the corridors and dormitories; he would look out for the dirtiest work that others shirked, and would do it; when building was going on in the convent he would carry up the stones and mortar; if anyone protested, declaring that such work did not become a priest, he would only reply:

"What else can Brother Ass do?"

And when he got Brother Ass alone in his cell, he would beat him to make him work harder.

But now began that wonderful experience the like of which is scarcely to be paralleled in the life of any other saint. It was first in his prayer. Joseph's absent-mindedness, from his childhood upwards, had not been only a natural weakness; it was due, in great part, to a wonderful gift of seeing God and the supernatural in everything about him, and he would become lost in the wonder of it all. Now when he was a friar, and a priest besides, the vision grew stronger; it seemed easier for him to see God indwelling in His creation than the material creation in which he dwelt. The realisation became to him so vivid, so engrossing, that he would spend whole days lost in its fascination, and only an order from his superiors could bring him back to earth. It would come suddenly upon him anywhere; as it were from out of space the eyes of God would look at him, or on the face of nature the hand of God would be seen at work, disposing all things. Joseph would stand still, exactly as the vision caught him, fixed as a statue, insensible as a stone, and nothing could move him. The brethren would use pins and burning embers to recall him to his senses, but nothing could he feel. When he did revive and saw what had happened, he would call these visitations fits of giddiness, and ask them not to burn him again. Once a prelate, who had come to see him on some business, noticed that his hands were covered with sores. Joseph could not hide them, nor could he hide the truth, but he had an explanation ready.

"See, Father, what the brethren have to do to me when the fits of giddiness come on. They have to burn my hands, they have to cut my fingers, that is what they have to do."

And Joseph laughed, as he so often laughed; but we suspect that it was laughter keeping back tears.

Then there came another visitation. In the midst of these ecstasies Joseph would rise from the ground, and move about in the air. In the church especially this would come upon him; he would fly towards the altar or over it, or to a shrine on a special festival. In the refectory, during a meal, he would suddenly rise from the ground with a dish of food in his hands, much to the alarm of the brethren at table. When he was out in the country begging, suddenly he would fly into a tree. Once when some workmen were labouring to plant a huge stone cross in its socket, Joseph rose above them, took up the cross and placed it in the socket for them. A little thing would suffice to bring about these levitations; a word of praise of the Creator and His creature, of the beauty of the sky or of the trees on the roadside, and away Joseph would go.

Along with this went a power over nature, over the birds and beasts of the field, surpassing even that of his Father, St. Francis of Assisi; and Joseph used his power playfully, as St. Francis used it. There was a convent of nuns not far from the monastery, where Joseph sometimes called for alms. One day, when they had been good to him, he told them with a laugh that in return for their kindness he would send them a bird to help them in their singing. The next time they went to office, in flew a sparrow by the window. All the time they sang he sang too; when the office was over he flew away again. And so it happened every day; morning and evening the sparrow was there, as regular as any nun. But one day a sister, passing him by, gave him a push with her hand; the sparrow flew out at once and did not return any more. When next Joseph came to the convent, the sisters told him that the sparrow was gone, but they did not tell him the reason.

"He is gone, and quite right," said Joseph; "he did not come to you to be insulted."

However, he promised he would make amends to the sparrow; and in due time he appeared again, and joined in the office as before.

But that does not end the story of the sparrow. He would become so familiar that the nuns could play with him; one of them tied a tiny bell to his foot. All went well till Maundy Thursday; on that day he did not appear, nor during the rest of Holy Week. When Joseph called on Holy Saturday to receive his Easter offering, they told him the sparrow had gone.

"No wonder," answered Joseph, "I gave him to you to join in your music; you should not have made him a bellringer. Bells are not rung during these days of Holy Week. But I will see that he returns."

And he did. The sparrow returned, and did not leave again so long as Joseph remained in the neighbourhood.

Let us take another story from the many that are found in the life of this servant whom God loved. Joseph had a special interest in the shepherds of the neighbourhood; with people of that class he was always most at home. It was his custom to meet them every Saturday in a little chapel at a corner of the monastery grounds, and there recite with them the Litany of Our Lady and other prayers. His congregation was usually a large one, swelled by people from the village. One Saturday Joseph went to the chapel as usual, and found not a soul there. It was harvest time; shepherds and villagers were out in the meadows and had forgotten to tell him that that day they could not come. Joseph, knowing nothing of the reason, talked to himself about the fickleness of men in the service of God. As he spoke he looked down the valley in the distance. The sheep were in the fields, but there were no shepherds; only a few children to tend them. Joseph raised his voice.

"Sheep of God," he cried, "come to me. Come and honour the Mother of God, who is also your Mother."

Immediately the sheep all around looked up. They left their pasture, leaped over hedges and ditches, formed themselves into orderly companies, and gathered round Joseph at the chapel door. When all were assembled, Joseph knelt down and began:

"Kyrie eleison."

"Baa," answered the sheep.

"Christe eleison."

"Baa."

"Sancta Maria."

"Baa."

And so it went on till the litany was finished. Then Joseph stood and blessed his congregation; and the sheep went back to their pastures as if nothing unusual had happened.

Such were some of the stories the brethren had to tell one another of Joseph and his ways. There were many more, especially of miracles he wrought among the poor. He would touch blind eyes and they would see; he would lift up a sick child and it would be cured; he would write out the benediction of St. Francis and it would be passed round a village and work wonders. But there were some among the brethren, as there are always and everywhere, who did not believe in these things. They were incredible, they were impossible, they could not have occurred as the evidence declared. Besides, Joseph was not the kind of person to whom such things would happen; he had too many faults to be a saint, he lacked all kinds of virtues, he was generally a trouble in the community. Therefore he was an impostor, a maker of mischief, who "stirred up the people, beginning from Galilee even to that place." He was reported to the Vicar General; the Vicar General believed what was said, and Joseph was called to stand his trial before the inquisitors of Naples. The inquisitors examined him; after close testing they were unable to convict him of anything. Still they would not dismiss him; his case was at least doubtful, and they sent him for further examination to the General of the Order in Rome. The General received him, at first, with little favour. Generals of religious orders have enough to do, and more than enough to give them trouble, without being tried by such subjects as Joseph. Moreover, Joseph never could say anything for himself; if superiors were hard on him he was tongue-tied and could only submit. But this very submission, in this case, was his saving. Father General saw his humility; he began to doubt whether all was true that was said against him. In the end he himself took him to see the Holy Father; and in the Pope's presence as, perhaps, might have been expected, Joseph was humiliated by having another of his "fits of giddiness."

But for all that, though nothing positive could be proved against him, during the rest of his life Joseph was submitted to a new kind of trial. It was the beginning of his Passion, and it lasted to the end. The explanation is not quite clear. It may have been that the tribunal of the Inquisition doubted whether it was safe to allow him, with his strange power, and his strange character, to wander about at will. It was not certain whence these powers came; devotees might make of them more than they ought; yet others might take scandal at Joseph's peculiar ways; many were the arguments adduced to make it clear that he must be piously but firmly kept in safe custody. The Inquisition of Perugia received a peremptory order to take him at once from his own monastery and to hand him over to the Father Guardian of a Capuchin convent, hidden away among the hills, there to be kept in the strictest seclusion. For a moment, when he heard the sentence, Joseph shivered. "Have I to go to prison?" he asked, as if he had been condemned. But in an instant he recovered. He knelt down and kissed the Inquisitor's feet; then got into the carriage, smiling as usual as if nothing had happened.

Arrived at the convent, Joseph was treated with the strictest rigour. Under pain of excommunication he was forbidden to speak to anyone, except the religious around him. He was not permitted to write letters or receive them; he might not leave the convent enclosure; all intercourse with the outside world was cut off. Why all this was done Joseph did not know, and he never asked; but he wondered above all why he had been taken from his own Conventuals and delivered over to the Capuchins.

Nevertheless, in spite of all this care, he could not be hidden. In course of time it became known where he had been spirited away; and pilgrims who had learnt to revere him came to the place for the privilege of hearing his mass. He was transferred to another hiding-place, where again the same regulations were enforced. Here the same thing occurred, and once more he was taken away. For the last ten years of his life he seems to have lived virtually in prison, always being kept away from the crowds who persisted in seeking the man they proclaimed to be a saint.

Meanwhile within his places of imprisonment the same wonderful experiences continued. He would be shut up in his cell and he would see things going on elsewhere. He would kneel down to pray before a statue in the garden, and the friars would see him rise in the air, still in a kneeling position. They would come to speak to him, and would be surprised that he read their thoughts before they spoke; sometimes he would read there more than they wished him to know. One morning he came down to the church to say mass, and announced to the brethren about him that the Pope had died during the night. Another time he made the same announcement; the occasions were the deaths of Urban VIII and Innocent X.

In 1657, six years before his death, Joseph was given back to his own Conventuals, and by them was transferred to another place of seclusion, from which he never emerged. The regulations were the same, the surveillance, if anything, was stricter than ever. He was assigned a tiny cell apart from the community, and a little chapel in which he might say his mass apart from others. Indeed, scarcely anything else could be done. For years before he was secluded it had been impossible to admit him to office with

the rest of the community; his ecstasies had become so frequent, and so continuous, as to throw all into disorder. For
the same reason he had been made to take his meals apart.
Now, in his last home, he was left to himself; and he lived,
this dull man whom no one could teach, and no one
wanted, almost continually wrapt up in the vision of that
which no man can express in words.

But the time at last came for his release. When, in 1657,
Joseph had been taken to his last place of confinement, he
had said he would never leave it. He added one thing more
for a sign. He told his companions that the first day on
which he failed to receive communion would be the day
on which he would die. And so it came about. On August
10, 1663, he was seized with an intermittent fever. So long
as it was only intermittent he continued to rise every morning to say mass. The last day was the feast of the Assump-
tion; on that day, says the Act of his canonisation, he had
ecstasies and experiences surpassing anything he had ever
had before. Then he was compelled to take to his bed; but
still he persisted in hearing mass when he could, and never
missed communion. He became worse, and extreme unc-
tion was administered. When he had received it, he had
one request to make; it was that his body should be buried
in some out-of-the-way corner, and that it should be forgotten where it was laid. He fell into his agony. There came
constantly to his lips the words of St. Paul: *Cupio dissolvi
et esse cum Christo*. Someone at the bedside spoke to him
of the love of God; he cried out: "Say that again, say that
again!" He pronounced the Holy Name of Jesus. He added:
"Praised be God! Blessed be God! May the holy will of
God be done!" The old laughter seemed to come back to
his face; those around could scarcely resist the contagion.
And so he died. It was September 18, 1663. He was just
sixty years of age.

BLESSED CLAUDE
DE LA COLOMBIÈRE

1641–1682

The beautification of Blessed Claude de La Colombière cannot be without interest to English Catholics, more especially to Catholics in London. Anyone passing St. James's Palace may recall that for two years he lived there, in the last days of Charles II; therefore at that time he must often have been seen, passing down Pall Mall or up St. James's Street, a singular figure in such a gay world, tolerated because he was a Frenchman, protected because he was the official chaplain of Mary of Modena, the wife of James, then Duke of York. But still more should his memory be dear to English Catholic hearts because it is to him that we owe it that, even in those times of trouble, the first formal petition for the establishment of the Feast of the Sacred Heart was sent to Rome from London. We may add another reason; unless we are mistaken Claude de La Colombière is the last resident in England not a martyr who has been beatified. On that account we would claim him as one of ourselves, closely allied with our martyrs.

And yet, when we come to study his career, there is singularly little to be said about him; indeed one may assert that he has been remembered more because of his connection with the name of another than on his own account. Had he never come across St. Margaret Mary he might never have been known, any more than Bernadette would

have been known, had it not been for the apparitions at
Lourdes. Nor, when he is known, is it easy at first to discover the sanctity in its highest degree which was his. There
is little to show us that any of his contemporaries and
friends looked on him as anything more than an excellent
religious, and even that on some accounts might have
seemed to need qualification. There are saints whom no
man would discover if God did not discover them for him;
one of these was La Colombière. There are saints who have
never dreamt they were saints; it would seem that of no
one could this be more truly said than of him.

Claude de La Colombière was one of a family of seven
children, two of whom died young, four of the rest em-
braced the religious life or the priesthood; of his childhood
we know practically nothing. At the age of nine he went
to a Jesuit school; almost all we know of his schooldays is
that he "showed ability"; a remark that will have been
made of many of his companions. When he was seventeen
he entered the Jesuit noviciate; we are told that he had
"a horrible aversion to the life he chose", but he is not
the only novice who has felt the same. He passed through
his course of training very much as any other scholastic;
if during his theology he was at the same time appointed
tutor to the children of Colbert this was nothing exceptional. By an indiscretion of his own he lost that post; this
threw him back into the colleges, where he held offices
suited to one of rather more than average ability, but not
of themselves suggestive of anything exceptional, whether
in nature or in grace. He then made his third year of probation; after which, at the age of thirty-five, he was sent as
superior to the residence at Paray-le-Monial. During his
college days he had taught rhetoric, and had shown a gift
for preaching; at the same time he was delicate in physique,
and incapable of excessive work. It would seem that these
two circumstances had decided his appointment to Paray,
where he could exercise his talent without undue pressure
or labour.

His work in Paray was such as might have been expected

of a good religious, little more. He took a lively interest in the little Jesuit school that was under him; he founded a sodality for men; he helped in the founding of a hospital; he preached with apparently average success; he was sought for as a confessor and a director of souls; to the outside world that appears to have been all. But he was also extraordinary confessor to the Visitation nuns of Paray, and in that convent at the moment Sister Margaret Mary Alacoque was causing anxiety. Naturally Father de La Colombière soon came across her. He studied her case and at once, against the opinion of others, he espoused her cause; he was rewarded, perhaps not altogether at first to his liking, by being told by the saint that he was the one appointed by Our Lord to be her chief support in the task imposed upon her. Still he did not shrink. He became her staunch friend and adviser; if we may judge from notes written in his journal more than two years later, he accepted this responsibility as a further motive compelling him to aim at the highest sanctity.

He lived at Paray-le-Monial only eighteen months, after which he was appointed chaplain to the Duchess of York, daughter of the Duke of Modena, in London. There he lived, in St. James's Palace, for two years, a lonely and cramped life, but, if we may judge from his letters, not without the fruit which an earnest priest in such a situation might have been expected to reap. At the end of that time he was betrayed by a Frenchman whom he thought he had converted. He was accused of reconciling heretics, and of speaking against the king; it was the year of the Titus Oates "Plot," and La Colombière, a Jesuit, and living in the household of the Duke of York, must have seemed a likely source of information. He was thrown into prison, cross-examined many times, but clearly knew nothing of what was said to be going on; at length, being a Frenchman, he was banished from the country. But before he could leave his health broke down; the hardships of his prison, added to the rigour of the English climate, had affected his lungs, and he suffered a serious haemorrhage. As soon as he was able he returned to France; there he was given light work as spiritual father in the college of Lyons. But he never recovered. He was removed to Paray in the hope that the climate might suit him better; and there he died, on February 15th, 1682, having just completed his forty-first year. A good man, so his brethren thought, but not exactly what was usually ranked as a saint. He had worked no miracles; he had written no books; he had done nothing in particular. His health had prevented him from using his talents as they might have been used; he had lived only six years from his probation, and two of those had been spent in London, hidden away, unknown to his fellow-religious, bearing no fruit that could be seen. He was buried as a good man might have been expected to be buried, with the usual becoming ceremony; perhaps there were those among the mourners who regretted that here was another good life thrown away.

But when he was gone two precious documents were found among his papers. It was true Sister Margaret Mary had always spoken of him as something exceptional, and after his death revered him as a saint; but this was put down to her natural enthusiasm, perhaps a little to her biased judgment, a matter of fidelity to the memory of one who had been her staunch support and champion. But these two documents proved that she was right. None but a man with the highest ideals could have written them; if he had lived up to the standard they laid down, then without a doubt he had lived a life of heroic sanctity. And when his brethren came to reflect upon it, gradually they saw that he had. Gradually his name was dissociated from that of St. Margaret Mary, and the devotion of which she constituted him the first apostle; it was found that it represented one who on his own account deserved a place in the ranks of the Church's saints.

Beneath these great ideals, is it possible to trace the natural man on which they are built? We think it is. Colombière has written his double self-analysis, one during his third year of probation, the other during a retreat he made in England, with such simplicity and accurate attention to detail that we are able to infer the things he has omitted without much fear of mistake. And the picture we would draw is something of this kind. By nature Colombière was a man given to despondency, to self-mistrust leading almost to despair, even as at one time was his immediate predecessor, to whom he had so great a devotion, St. Francis de Sales. He had a keen appreciation of art and literature, with which there usually goes great sensitiveness of soul; he felt things keenly, above all his own apparent failures, even in the little things of life. Though once or twice he breaks out in expressions of devotion, yet as a rule his prayer was dry and arid; with all his aspirations after sanctity, he can only resign himself to the commonest planes of the spiritual life and look for perfection in that resignation. Behind all this, the placid exterior, interpreted by his contemporaries, and even by modern biographers, as a sign of placidity within, in matter of fact concealed a soul unceasingly troubled by a whirl of temptation, and of passions which he had need of every grace to resist.

It is in this light that we would read and interpret the three or four characteristics of his sanctity; they were the outcome of the battle he found he had to fight, and of experience of himself, more than of any illumination from without. Margaret Mary had visions and ecstasies, Colombière had none. She was told what she had to do, even in the matter of her own perfection; Colombière had to discover all this by the painful sifting of himself. In the third year of probation he took a vow always to do the thing that was most perfect; we can see that the vow was taken, less because of any great light from above, more because of the trouble he found in battling with his own nature. Later he took another vow, to choose by preference, when the choice was allowed him, the thing that he most disliked; again we see in it the determined conquest of his sensitive nature, more than straining after sanctity. Throughout his life his ideal of prayer was, as it were, to have no ideal; to be content with what was given him, and not even to aspire to more; this was nothing else but the recognition of his common experience, and the determination to turn it into what profit he could. Lastly, in regard to sanctity itself he has language almost peculiarly his own. Much as his soul longed for it, he seemed to think that a nature like his could never attain to sublime perfection; he meets the apparently hopeless prospect by accepting as his goal just that standard which is appointed for him and no more. Of all the saints in the calendar of the Church few can have been less aware of their sanctity than was Colombière.

To illustrate these characteristics of our saint we have only to compare certain passages in which he expresses his own mind; from first to last there is a certain consistency which enables us to read what is going on beneath. Thus, on the seventh day of his Long Retreat he writes:

"On the seventh day, during the morning, I found myself attacked with thoughts of mistrust in regard to the aim in life which I am making for the future; I see in it hopeless difficulties. Any other life would seem to me easy to spend in the manner of a saint, so it appears to me, and the more austere, solitary, obscure, separated from all communication, so much the sweeter would it seem to me to be. Much as I dread the ordinary things of nature, such as imprisonment, continued sickness, death itself, all these appear to me pleasant in comparison with an everlasting fight against the surprises of worldliness and self-love, and of that death in life in the midst of the world. When I think on it all, it seems to me that life is going to be intolerably long, and that death will not come soon enough; I understand the words of St. Augustine: *Patienter vivit, et delectabiliter moritur.*"

So he wrote in 1674, when he was preparing for his vow of perfection. Three years later, during a retreat in England, we find him recalling the vow with satisfaction, saying he looks on it as "the greatest grace I have ever received in all my life"; nevertheless the next note is this:

"I am made miserable on a matter of which I cannot speak; my imagination is mad and extravagant. All the passions toss my heart about; there scarcely passes a day but all, one after another, stir in me the most unruly emotions. Sometimes they are real things that rouse me, sometimes they are pure imaginations. It is true that by the mercy of God I endure all this without contributing much to it of myself and without consenting to it; still, at any moment I catch these foolish passions stirring up this poor heart. My self-love flies from corner to corner, and is never without a hiding-place; I feel very sorry for myself. Still I do not lose my temper, I do not let myself feel annoyed; what would be the use? I ask God to let me know what I ought to do to serve Him and to purify myself; but I am resolved to wait in peace till it pleases Him to work this miracle, for I am quite convinced that He alone can do it: *Quis potest facere mundum de immundo conceptum semine, nisi tu qui solus es?*" (Job xv, 4).

Passages parallel to these might be multiplied. They tell with sufficient clearness the struggle that was always going on with an unruly nature; their proximity to the places where he speaks of the vow makes one suspect that the two are connected. In like manner we may judge of his prayer. It is true that in many places he speaks of his attraction for prayer; nevertheless no less often does he tell us of his dryness, always he emphasizes that his prayer is of the common sort, and that he does not wish it to be otherwise. There is no more striking summary of his mind than the following, taken from the notes of his retreat in 1674.

"Since by the mercy of God I feel myself somewhat drawn to prayer, I have asked of God, with a large heart, through the intercession of the Blessed Virgin, that He would give me the grace to love this holy exercise more and more, unto the hour of my death. It is the one means for our purification, the one way to union with God, the one channel by which God may unite Himself with us, that

He may do anything with us for His glory. To obtain the virtues of an apostle we must pray; to make them of use to our neighbour we must pray; to prevent our losing them while we use them in His service we must pray. The counsel, or rather the commandment: Pray always, seems to me extremely sweet and by no means impossible. It secures the practice of the presence of God; I wish, with the help of Our Lord, to endeavour to follow it. We are always in need of God, then we need to pray always; the more we pray the more we please Him, and the more we receive. I do not ask for those delights in prayer which God gives to whom He will; I am not worthy of them, I have not strength enough to bear them. Extraordinary graces are not good for me; to give them to me would be to build on sand, it would only be pouring precious liquor into a leaking hogshead which can hold nothing. I ask of God only a solid, simple manner of prayer, which may give Him glory and will not puff me up; dryness and desolation, accompanied with His grace, are very good for me, so it seems. Then I make acts of the best kind, and with satisfaction; then I make efforts against my evil disposition, I try to be faithful to God, etc."

Shortly afterwards he concludes:

"Above all things I am resigned to be sanctified by the way that God shall please, by the absence of all sensible delight, if He wishes it so to be, by interior trials, by continual combat with my passions."

There seems to be no evidence that he ever deviated from this path, or rose beyond the prayer of simplicity. In the retreat of 1677 he confesses that he finds little help in points for meditation, and decides to fall back upon his favourite method of the practice of the presence of God; that is all. But that is an experience of many souls of prayer, who nevertheless are far from being saints; it is foreseen and prepared for by every writer on prayer, within the Society of Jesus as well as without.

With all this as a background we may well now ask ourselves what was the characteristic of his sanctity. It has already been suggested that the need of unceasing battle with himself led him to make first one heroic vow and then another; the faithful fulfilment of those vows meant the making of a saint. But as a first characteristic trait we would notice Colombière's childlike simplicity; to the end he remained a child. This is manifest enough in the spontaneous way he writes of himself; it is manifest no less in his correspondence, in the stories he narrates, in the simplicity of his advice, in the confidence he shows towards his correspondents. But most of all does it appear in his attitude towards St. Margaret Mary. It was simplicity of soul that enabled him to understand her from the first; the same simplicity made him think of her, and speak of her with the greatest reverence; what she told him of himself he took as perhaps his chief source of encouragement. For example, what can be more simply childlike than the following? He has been speaking of his former temptation to vainglory and human respect:

"Formerly (he says) I was so strongly obsessed with this temptation, that it sapped all my courage, and made me almost lose all hope of saving my own soul while thinking of the souls of others. So strong was it that if I had been free I do not doubt that I would have passed my days in solitude."

Then naïvely he goes on:

"This temptation began to weaken from a word which N.N. [meaning St. Margaret Mary] spoke to me one day. For once when she told me that while praying to God for me, Our Lord had given her to understand that my soul was dear to Him, and that He would take particular care of it, I answered her: 'Alas! N.N., how can this agree with what I feel within myself? Could Our Lord love anyone as vain as I am, one whose only object is to please men, and to win consideration from them, one who is steeped in human respect?'—'O my Father,' she replied, 'all this does not really belong to you.' It is true that this single word of assurance gave me peace; from that time I troubled myself less about these temptations, and they grew weaker and less frequent."

In other places Colombière falls back for his own encouragement on the words of St. Margaret Mary. Evidently, if he was her main support, she in her turn did no less for him. So simple, and childlike, and dependent was this guide of other souls.

Nevertheless we have not yet touched upon the quality which seems to us most characteristic of Colombière. With a nature given to mistrust of itself and consequent despondency, with a physique which would never permit him to labour to the extent of his desires, placed in situations which invariably seemed to go wrong, or to give him little scope for his zeal, lastly with a spiritual experience in his soul which was more often desolate than consoling, it is no wonder that there grew within him an unbounded confidence in God, as the one mainstay on which he could rely. He speaks of trust in superiors, of openness with his spiritual fathers, of simplicity in dealing with others, of his love of friendship; but all these are treated more as external signs of self-conquest and charity, they are less considered as supports to himself. When he speaks of confidence in God it is quite different. He sees his sins, but the mercy of God is infinite, and he will not despair. He looks up to God in His majesty, to his Lord in the Blessed Sacrament, to the indwelling of God in the human soul, to the union of the heart of man with the heart of Our Lord by complete surrender; and he flings himself blindly into the arms of God to find there perfect peace. Nowhere does he write with more self-revelation than on the last day of his retreat in England. The passage is a summary of his life; we have but to read between the lines, giving each phrase its full value, and we seem to know Colombière well.

"On this eighth day (he writes) I seem to have found a great treasure, if only I can profit by it. It is a firm confidence in God, founded on His infinite goodness, and on the experience I have had that He never fails us in our needs. More than that, I find in the memoir which was given to me when I left France, that He promises to be my strength in proportion to the trust which I place in Him. Therefore I am resolved to put no limit to my trust, and to spread it out to everything. It seems to me that I ought to make use of Our Lord as an armour which covers me all about, by means of which I shall resist every device of my enemies. You shall then be my strength, O my God! You shall be my guide, my director, my counsellor, my patience, my knowledge, my peace, my justice, and my prudence. I will have recourse to you in my temptations, in my dryness, in my repugnances, in my weariness, in my fears; or rather I will no longer fear either the illusions or the tricks of the demon, nor my own weakness, my indiscretions, not even my mistrust of myself. For you must be my strength in all my crosses; you promise me that this you will be in proportion to my confidence. And wonderful indeed it is, O my God, that at the same time that you impose this condition, it seems to me that you give me the confidence wherewith to fulfil it. May you be eternally loved and praised by all creatures, O my very loving Lord! If you were not my strength, alas! what would I do? But since you are, you assure me that you are, what shall I not do for your glory? *Omnia possum in eo qui me confortat.* You are everywhere in me, and I in you; then in whatever situation I may find myself, in whatever peril whatever enemy may rise up against me, I have my support always with me. This thought alone can in a moment scatter all my trials, above all those uprisings of nature which at times I find so strong, and which in spite of myself, make me fear for my perseverance, and tremble at the sight of the perfect emptiness in which it has pleased God to place me."

Could St. Augustine be more transparent? When in his sermons we hear Colombière crying out that even were he in mortal sin he would still never doubt that God would save him, we understand the source of his unbounded hope. He was a very human being indeed; perhaps this was the reason why he was chosen before others to be the apostle of the human Heart of Jesus Christ. "Come to me all you that labour and are burdened, and I will refresh you. . . . Learn of me, because I am meek and humble of heart. . . . You shall find rest for your souls." It would be hard to find a more perfect fulfilment of this prophecy than is found in the soul of Claude de La Colombière.

&

ST. BENEDICT JOSEPH LABRE
THE BEGGAR SAINT

1748–1783

&

There is no condition of life which the grace of God has not sanctified; this is the first reflection that must rise in the mind of anyone who studies the history of Benedict Joseph Labre. He died a beggar in Rome in 1783. Within a year of his death his reputation for sanctity had spread, it would seem, throughout Europe. The man and his reputed miracles were being discussed in London papers before the end of 1784. During that year the first authentic life of him appeared, from the pen of his confessor; it was written, as the author expressly states in the preface, because so many tales were being told about him. In 1785 an abridged translation was published in London; surely a remarkable witness, when we consider the place and the times—it was only five years after the Gordon riots—to the interest his name had aroused. We wonder in our own day at the rapidity with which the name of St. Thérèse of Lisieux has spread over the Christian world; though St. Benedict's actual canonisation has taken a longer time, nevertheless his cultus spread more quickly, and that in spite of the revolutionary troubles of those days, and the difficulties of communication. Rousseau and Voltaire had died five years before; ten years later came the execution of Louis XVI, and the massacres of the French Revolution were at their height. In studying the life of Benedict Joseph Labre these dates cannot be without their significance.

Benedict from the beginning of his days was nothing if not original. His originality consisted mainly in this, that he saw more in life than others saw, and what he saw made him long to sit apart from it; it gave him a disgust, even to sickness, for things with which ordinary men seem to be contented. Other men wanted money, and the things that money could buy; Benedict never had any use for either. Other men willingly became the slaves of fashion and convention; Benedict reacted against it all, preferring at any cost to be free. He preferred to live his life untrammelled, to tramp about the world where he would—what was it made for but to trample on?—to go up and down, a pure soul of nature, without any artificial garnish, just being what God made him, and taking every day what God gave him, in the end giving back to God that same being, perfect, unhampered, untainted.

But it was not all at once that Benedict discovered his vocation; on the contrary, before he reached it he had a long way to go, making many attempts and meeting with many failures. He was born not far from Boulogne, the eldest of a family of fifteen children, and hence belonged to a household whose members had perforce to look very much after themselves. From the first, if you had met him, you would have said he was different from others of his class. The portrait drawn of him by his two chief biographers seems to set before us one of those quiet, meditative youths, not easy to fathom, unable to express themselves, easily misunderstood, who seem to stand aside from life, looking on instead of taking their part in it; one of those with whom you would wish to be friends yet cannot become intimate; cheerful always (the biographers are emphatic about this), yet with a touch of melancholy; whom women notice, yet do not venture too near; a puzzle to most who meet them, yet instinctively revered; by some voted "deep" and not trusted, while others, almost without reflecting on it, know that they can trust them with their very inmost souls.

Benedict had good parents, living in a comfortable state of life; their great ambition was that from their many children one at least should become a priest. Benedict, being the quiet boy he was, soon became the one on whom their hopes settled; and they spared no pains to have him educated to that end. He chanced to have an uncle, a parish priest, living some distance from his family home; this uncle gladly received him, and undertook his early education for the priesthood. Here for a time Benedict settled down, learning Latin and studying Scripture. He was happy enough, though his originality of mind dragged against him. His Latin was a bore, and he did not make much of it, but the Scriptures he loved. On the other hand, the poor in the lanes had a strange attraction for him; they were pure nature, without much of the convention that he so disliked; and he was often with them, and regularly emptied his pockets among them. Besides, he had a way of wandering off to the queerest places, mixing with the queerest people, ending up with long meditations in his uncle's church before the Blessed Sacrament.

But in spite of these long meditations, Benedict's uncle was by no means sure that with a character such as his, and with his wandering propensity, he would end as a priest. Meanwhile the thought came to Benedict himself that he would be a Trappist; the originality of their life, with its ideals the exact contrary to those of ordinary convention, seemed to him exactly like his own. He applied to his uncle; his uncle put him off by referring him to his parents; his parents would have none of it, and told him he must wait till he grew older. At the time of this first attempt Benedict was about sixteen years of age.

He remained some two years longer with his priest-uncle, who continued to have his doubts about him. While he was still trying to make up his mind, when Benedict was about eighteen, an epidemic fell upon the city, and uncle and nephew busied themselves in the service of the sick.

The division of labour was striking; while the uncle, as became a priest, took care of the souls and bodies of the
people, Benedict went to and fro caring for the cattle. He
cleaned their stalls and fed them; the chronicler tells the
story as if, in spite of the epidemic, which had no fears
for him, Benedict were by no means loth to exchange this
life of a farm labourer for that of a student under his uncle's roof.

But a still greater change was pending. Among the last
victims of the epidemic was the uncle himself, and his
death left Benedict without a home. But this did not seem
to trouble him; Benedict was one of those who seldom show
trouble about anything. He had already developed that peculiar craving to do without whatever he could; and now
that Providence had deprived him of a home he began to
think that he might do without that as well. But what was
he to do? How was he to live? At first he had thought that
his natural aloofness from the ordinary ways of men meant
that he should be a monk. His family had put him off, but
why should he not try again? He was older now, arrived
at an age when young men ordinarily decide their vocations;
this time, he said to himself, he would not be so easily
prevented.

Benedict returned to his family with his mind made up.
He loved his parents—we have later abundant evidence of
that; natures like his have usually unfathomed depths of
love within them which they cannot show. He would not
go without their consent. He asked, and again they refused;
his mother first, and then all the rest of the household with
her. But he held on in his resolution, till at length in despair they surrendered, and Benedict set off with a glad
heart in the direction of La Trappe.

He arrived there only to be disappointed. The abbey at
which he applied had suffered much of late from the admission of candidates whose constitutions were unfitted for
the rigour of the life; in consequence the monks had passed
a resolution to admit no more unless they were absolutely
sound in body. Benedict did not come up to their require-

ments. He was under age; he was too delicate; he had no
special recommendations. They would make no exception,
especially so soon after the rule had been made. Benedict
was sent away, and returned to his family, and all they
said to him was: "We told you so."

Still he would not surrender. For a time he went to live
with another parish priest, a distant relative, that he might
continue his studies, and above all perfect himself in Latin.
But the craving to go away would not leave him. If the
Trappists would not have him, perhaps the Carthusians
would. At least he could try. Once more he told his parents
of his wish, and again, more than ever, they opposed him.
They showed him how his first failure was a proof that he
would fail again; how he was throwing away a certain future
for a shadow; how those best able to judge were all against
him; how with his exceptional education he might do so
much good elsewhere. Still he would have his way, and one
day, when he had won a consent from his parents that at
least he might try, he went off to ask for admission among
the Carthusians of Montreuil. But here again he met with
the same response. The monks were very kind, as Carthusians always are; they showed him every mark of affection,
but they told him as well that he had no vocation for them.
He was still too young to take up such a life; he had not
done so much as a year of philosophy; he knew nothing of
plain chant; without these he could not be admitted among
them.

Benedict went off, but this time he did not return
straight home. If one Carthusian monastery would not
have him, perhaps another would. There was one at Longuenesse; he was told that there they were in need of
subjects, and postulants were more easily admitted. He
tramped off to Longuenesse and applied; to his joy the
monks agreed to give him a trial. But the trial did not last
long. Benedict did his best to reconcile himself to the life,
but it was all in vain. Strange to say, the very confinement,
the one thing he had longed for, wore him down. The solitude, instead of giving him the peace he sought, seemed

only to fill him with darkness and despair. The monks grew uneasy; they feared for the brain of this odd young man; they told him he had no vocation and he was dismissed.

Benedict came home again, but his resolution was in no way shaken. His mother, naturally more than ever convinced that she was right, left no stone unturned to win him from his foolish fancy. Friends and neighbours joined in; they blamed him for his obstinacy, they accused him of refusing to recognise the obvious will of God, they called him unsociable, uncharitable, selfish, unwilling to shoulder the burden of life like other young men of his class. Still, in spite of all they said, Benedict held on. He could not defend himself; nevertheless he knew that he was right, and that he was following a star which would lead him to his goal at last. Since the Carthusians had said that he could not be received among them because he knew no philosophy or plain chant, that a year's course in these was essential, he found someone willing to teach him; and much as he disliked the study, he persevered for the year as he had been told. Then he applied once more at Montreuil. The conditions had been fulfilled; he was now older and his health had been better; he had proved his constancy by this test imposed upon him; though many of the monks shook their heads, still they could see that this persistent youth would never be content till he had been given another trial, and they received him.

But the result was again the same. He struggled bravely on with the life, but he began to shrink to a shadow. The rule enjoined quiet in his cell, and he could not keep still. After six weeks of trial the monks had to tell him that he was not designed for them, and asked him to go. He went, but this time not home; he made up his mind never to go home any more. He would try the Trappists again or some other confined Order; perhaps he would have to go from monastery to monastery till at last he found peace, but he would persevere. At any rate he would no longer trouble, or be a burden to, his parents or his family. On the road, after he had been dismissed from Montreuil, he wrote a letter to his parents; it is proof enough that with all his strange ways he had a very wide place in his heart for those he dearly loved.

"My dear Father and Mother,

"This is to tell you that the Carthusians have judged me not a proper person for their state of life, and I quitted their house on the second day of October.—I now intend to go to La Trappe, the place which I have so long and so earnestly desired. I beg your pardon for all my acts of disobedience, and for all the uneasiness which I have at any time caused you.—By the grace of God I shall henceforth put you to no further expense, nor shall I give you any more trouble.—I assure you that you are now rid of me. I have indeed cost you much; but be assured that, by the grace of God, I will make the best use of, and reap benefits from, all that you have done for me.—Give me your blessing, and I will never again be a cause of trouble to you. —I very much hope to be received at La Trappe; but if I should fail there, I am told that at the Abbey of Sept Fonts they are less severe, and will receive candidates like me. But I think I shall be received at La Trappe."

With hopes such as these he came to La Trappe and again was disappointed; the good monks declined even to reconsider his case. But he went on to Sept Fonts, as he had said he would in his letter, and there was accepted; for the third time he settled down to test his vocation as a monk. The trial lasted only eight months. He seems to have been happier here than anywhere before, yet in another sense he was far from happy. This youth with a passion for giving up everything, found that even in a Trappist monastery he could not give up enough. He craved to be yet more poor than a Trappist, he craved to be yet more starving; and what with his longing to give away more, and his efforts to be the poorest of the poor, he began to shrink to a mere skeleton, as he had done before at Montreuil. Added to this he fell ill, and was disabled for two months. Once more the community grew anxious; it was only too clear that he would never do for them. As soon as he was well enough to take the road he was told that he must go, that the strict life of the Trappist was too much for him; and with a "God's will be done" on his lips, and some letters of recommendation in his pocket, Benedict again passed out of the monastery door, into a world that hurt him.

Nevertheless in those few months he had begun at last to discover his true vocation. Though the longing for the monastic life did not entirely leave him, still he was beginning to see that there was now little hope of his being able to embrace it in the ordinary way. He was unlike other men; he must take the consequences and he would. He could not be a monk like others; then he would be one after his own manner. He could not live in the confinement of a monastery; then the whole world should be his cloister. There he would live, a lonely life with God, the loneliest of lonely men, the outcast of outcasts, the most pitied of all pitiful creatures, "a worm and no man, the reproach of men, and the outcast of the people." He would be a tramp, God's own poor man, depending on whatever men gave him from day to day, a pilgrim to heaven for the remainder of his life. He was twenty-five years of age.

He set off on his journey, with Rome as his first objective, a long cloak covering him, tied with a rope round the waist, a cross on his breast, a large pair of beads round his neck; his feet were partly covered with substitutes for shoes, carefully prepared, one might have thought, to let in water and stones. In this dress he braved every kind of weather, rain and snow, heat and the bitterest cold; he faced and endured it all without ever wincing or asking for a change. Over his shoulder he carried an old sack in which were all his belongings; chief among these were a bible and prayer-book. He ate whatever men gave him; if they gave him nothing he looked to see what he could find on the roadside. He refused to take thought for the morrow; if at any time he had more than sufficed for the day, he invariably gave it to another. Moreover, as a result of his poverty, Benedict soon ceased to be clean; the smell of Benedict was not always pleasant; even his confessor, who wrote his life, tells us very frankly that when Benedict came to confession he had to protect himself from vermin. Men of taste, even those who later came to look on him as a saint, could scarcely refrain from drawing aside when he came near them; and when they did, then was Benedict's heart full of joy. He had found what he wanted, his garden enclosed, his cloister that shut him off in the middle of the world; and the more he was spurned and ignored, the more did he lift up his eyes to God in thanksgiving.

With this light dawning on his soul, soon to grow into full noon, Benedict set out on his travels. He had gone through a long noviceship, living as it were between two worlds, one of which he would not have, while the other had repeatedly closed its doors to him; now at last his life proper had begun. We can discover his final decision in a letter he wrote to his parents from Piedmont, when he had now left France, and was half-way on his journey to Rome. It is a letter full of soul and warmth; it teems with sympathy and interest for others; there is not a word which implies bitterness or disappointment; the man who wrote it was a happy man, in no way disgruntled; evidently his only fear is that he may give pain to those he loved.

"My dear Father and Mother,

"You have heard that I have left the Abbey of Sept Fonts, and no doubt you are uneasy and desirous to know what route I have taken, and what kind of life I intend to adopt.—I must therefore acquaint you that I left Sept Fonts in July; I had a fever soon after I left, which lasted four days, and I am now on my way to Rome.—I have not travelled very fast since I left, on account of the excessive hot weather which there always is in the month of August in Piedmont, where I now am, and where, on account of a little complaint, I have been detained for three weeks in a hospital where I was kindly treated. In other respects I have been very well. There are in Italy many monasteries where the religious live very regular and austere lives; I design to enter into one of them, and I hope that God will prosper my design.—Do not make yourselves uneasy on my account. I will not fail to write to you from time to time. And I shall be glad to hear of you, and of my brothers and sisters; but this is not possible at present, because I am not yet settled in any fixed place; I will not fail to pray for you every day. I beg that you will pardon me for all the uneasiness that I have given you; and that you will give me your blessing, that God may favour my design.—I am very happy in having undertaken my present journey. I beg you will give my compliments to my grandmother, my grandfather, my aunts, my brother James and all my brothers and sisters, and my uncle Francis. I am going into a country which is a good one for travellers. I am obliged to pay the postage of this to France.

"Again I ask your blessing, and your pardon for all the uneasiness I have given you, and I subscribe myself,

"Your most affectionate son,

"BENEDICT JOSEPH LABRE.

"*Roziers in Piedmont, Aug. 31, 1770.*"

This was the last letter he appears to have written to his family. He had promised to write again; if he wrote the letter has perished. Indeed from this moment they seem to have lost sight of him altogether; the next they heard of him was fourteen years later, when his name was being blazoned all over Europe as that of a saint whose death had stirred all Rome. And he never heard from them. He had told them he could give them no address, because he had no fixed abode; from this time forward he never had one, except during the last years in Rome, and that for the most part was in a place where the post could scarcely have found him, as we shall see.

Except to give an idea of the nature and extent of his wanderings during the next six or seven years, it is needless to recall all the pilgrimages he made. They led him over mountains and through forests, into large cities and country villages; he slept under the open sky, or in whatever sheltered corner he could find, accepting in alms what sufficed for the day and no more, clothed with what men chose to give him, or rather with what they could induce him to accept; alone with God everywhere and wanting no one else. During this first journey he called on his way at Loreto and Assisi. Arrived in Rome, footsore and ill, he was admitted for three days into the French hospital; then for eight or nine months he lingered in the city, visiting all the holy places, known to no one, sleeping no one knows where. In September of the next year we find him again at Loreto; during the remaining months of that year, and through the winter, he seems to have visited all the sacred shrines in the kingdom of Naples. He was still there in February, 1772, after which he returned to Rome. In June he was again at Loreto; thence he set out on his tour to all the famous shrines of Europe. In 1773 he was tramping through Tuscany; in 1774, after another visit to Rome, he was in Burgundy; during the winter of that year he went to Einsiedeln in Switzerland, choosing the coldest season of the year for this visit to the mountain shrine. 1775, being the Jubilee year, he again spent in Rome; in 1776 he was making pilgrimages to the chief places of devotion in Germany. At the end of that year he settled down definitely in Rome, going away henceforth only on special pilgrimages, most of all to his favourite Loreto, which he did not fail to visit every year.

Naturally enough stories are recalled of the behaviour of this peculiar man on his journeys. He seems never to have had in his possession more than ten sous, or fivepence, at a time; when charitable people offered him more than sufficed for the day he invariably refused it. At Loreto, where he came to be known perhaps more than anywhere else, at first he lodged in a barn at some distance from the town; when compassionate friends found a room for him closer to the shrine, he refused it because he found it contained a bed. In Rome, as we have already hinted, his home for years was a hole he had discovered among the ruins of the Coliseum; from this retreat he made daily excursions to the various churches of the city. Except when he was ill he seldom begged; he was content with whatever the passers-by might give him of their own accord. Once a man, seeing him in his poverty, gave him a penny; Benedict thanked him, but finding it more than he needed, passed it on to another poor man close by. The donor, mistaking this for an act of contempt, supposing that Benedict had expected more, took his stick and gave him a beating. Benedict took the beating without a word. We have this on the evidence of the man himself, recorded in the enquiry after Benedict's death; it must be one instance of many of its kind.

But for the rest Benedict's life was one of continued prayer; he was a Trappist in a monastery of his own making. So far as he was able he kept perpetual silence; those who knew him afterwards related that he seemed to go whole months together without allowing his voice to be heard. He lived in retirement and solitude; he would accept no friend or companion; he would have only God; a few who had come to notice him, and who helped him when he would allow them, were invariably treated as patrons and benefactors, but no more. When a convent of nuns, at which occasionally he applied, had observed him, and began to show him more interest and respect, Benedict discovered their esteem and never went near them again. All his possessions were a few books of devotion and a wooden bowl; the latter had split, and he had kept it together with a piece of wire. He fasted and abstained continually, sometimes perforce, sometimes by chance; by constantly kneeling on the hard ground, or the stone floors of the churches, he developed sores on both knees. He deliberately tried to be despised and shunned, and when men could not refrain from showing contempt in their manner, then would Benedict's face light up with real joy. Let his confessor, who wrote his life a year after his death, describe his first meeting with him:

"In the month of June, 1782, just after I had celebrated mass in the church of St. Ignatius belonging to the Roman College, I noticed a man close beside me whose appearance at first sight was decidedly unpleasant and forbidding. His legs were only partially covered, his clothes were tied round his waist with an old cord. His hair was uncombed, he was ill-clad, and wrapped about in an old and ragged coat. In his outward appearance he seemed to be the most miserable beggar I had ever seen. Such was the spectacle of Benedict the first time I beheld him."

For what remains of Benedict's story we cannot do better than follow the guidance of this director. After the priest had finished his thanksgiving, on the occasion just mentioned, Benedict approached him and asked him to appoint a time when he would hear his general confession. The time and place were arranged. During the confession the priest was surprised, not only at the care with which it was made, but also at the knowledge his penitent showed of intricate points of theology. He concluded that, beggar though he was then, he had evidently seen better days; indeed he felt sure that he had once been a clerical student. He therefore interrupted the confession to ask whether he had ever studied divinity. "I, Father?" said Benedict. "No, I never studied divinity. I am only a poor ignorant beggar."

The confessor at once recognised that he was dealing with something unusual. He resolved to do for him all he could, and for the future to keep him carefully in mind.

As it has so often been in God's dealings with hidden saints whom He has willed that men should come at last to know, that apparently chance meeting was the means by which the memory of Benedict was saved. It took place in June, 1782; in April of the following year Benedict died. During those ten months the priest to whom he addressed himself had ample opportunity to watch him. As the weeks passed by he grew in wonder at the sanctity that lay beneath rags; and yet he tells us that, not a little fastidiously clean as he seems to have been himself, it never so much

as occurred to him to bid Benedict mend his ways. To hear
his confession cost him an effort, yet he never thought twice
about making that effort; only at times, for the sake of
others, the appointed place was out of the way.

He saw him last on the Friday before Holy Week, 1783,
when Benedict came to make his confession as usual. He
remarks that though always before Benedict had fixed the
day when he would come again, this time he made no appointment. The next the priest heard of him was that he
was dead, exactly a week later. But he was not surprised.
For some months before, when once he had come to know
Benedict and his way of life, he had wondered how he
lived. Apart from his austerities, and his invariable choice
of food that was least palatable, of late his body had begun
to develop sores and ulcers. The priest had spoken to him
on this last point, and had exhorted him at least to take
more care of his sores, but Benedict had taken little notice.
On his side, as the confessor could not but notice, and as
is common with saints as death draws nearer, the love of
God that was in him left him no desire to live any longer.

It came to Wednesday in Holy Week. Among the
churches which Benedict frequented none saw him more
than S. Maria dei Monti, not very far from the Coliseum.
In this church he usually heard mass every morning; in the
neighbourhood he was well known. On this day he had at-
tended the morning services; as he went out of the door,
about one in the afternoon, he was seen to fall on the steps.
Neighbours ran towards him. He asked for a glass of water,
but he could not lift himself up. A local butcher, who had
often been kind to Benedict, offered to have him carried
to his house, and Benedict agreed. They laid him on a bed,
as they thought, to rest; but it soon became clear that he
was dying. A priest was sent for; the Last Sacraments were
administered; but Benedict was too weak to receive Viati-
cum. The prayers for the dying were said; at the words:
"Holy Mary, pray for him," Benedict died, without a sigh
or a convulsion. It was the 16th of April, 1783: Benedict
was thirty-five years of age.

And now some remarkable things happened. His confessor and first biographer writes:

"Scarcely had this poor follower of Christ breathed his last when all at once the little children from the houses hard by filled the whole street with their noise, crying out with one accord: 'The Saint is dead, the Saint is dead.'—But presently after they were not only young children who published the sanctity of Benedict; all Rome soon joined in their cries, repeating the self-same words: 'A Saint is dead.' . . . Great numbers of persons who have been eminent for their holiness, and famous for their miracles, have ended the days of their mortal life in this city; but the death of none of them ever excited so rapid and lively an emotion in the midst of the people as the death of this poor beggar. This stirred a kind of universal commotion; for in the streets scarcely anything could be heard but these few words: 'There is a saint dead in Rome. Where is the house in which he has died?' "

Nor does this description seem to have been exaggerated. Not only was it written within a year of the event, so that anyone could bear witness to its truth; but we know that scarcely was Benedict dead before two churches were contending for the privilege of possessing his body. At length it was decided that it should be given to S. Maria dei Monti, which he had most frequented; and thither, on the Wednesday night, it was carried. So great was the crowd that the guard of police had to be doubled; a line of soldiers accompanied the body to the church; more honour could scarcely have been paid to a royal corpse. From the moment that it was laid there the church was thronged with mourners; the next day, Maundy Thursday, and again throughout Good Friday, it almost lay in state during all the Holy Week services. The throng all the time went on increasing, so that the Cardinal Vicar was moved to allow the body to remain unburied for four days. People of every rank and condition gathered there; at the feet of Benedict the Beggar all were made one. They buried him in the church, close beside the altar, on Easter Sunday afternoon; when the body was placed in the coffin it was remarked that it was soft and flexible, as of one who had but just been dead.

But the enthusiasm did not end with the funeral. Crowds continued to flock to the church, soldiers were called out to keep order. At length the expedient was tried of closing the church altogether for some days. It was of no avail; as soon as the church was re-opened the crowds came again, and continued coming for two months. Nothing like it had been seen before, even in Rome; if ever anyone was declared a saint by popular acclamation it was Benedict Joseph Labre, the beggar. Then the news spread abroad. Within a year the name of Benedict was known all over Europe. Lives of him began to appear, legends began to grow, miracles, true and false, were reported from all sides; it was to secure an authentic story, among many inventions, that his confessor was called upon to write the Life that we know.

Let us add one touching note. All this time the father and mother, brothers and sisters of Benedict were living in their home near Boulogne. For more than twelve years they had heard nothing of him; they had long since presumed that he was dead. Now, through these rumours, it dawned upon them very gradually that the saint of whom all the world was speaking was their son!

"My son was dead, and is come to life again; he was lost, and is found."

Image Books

... MAKING THE WORLD'S FINEST CATHOLIC LITERATURE AVAILABLE TO ALL

6

Image Books

... MAKING THE WORLD'S FINEST
CATHOLIC LITERATURE AVAILABLE TO ALL

ON THE TRUTH OF THE
CATHOLIC FAITH
*Summa Contra Gentiles Book II:
Creation. Newly translated, with
an Introduction and notes by
James F. Anderson* D27—95¢

ON THE TRUTH OF THE
CATHOLIC FAITH
*Summa Contra Gentiles Book
III: Providence. Newly trans-
lated, with an Introduction and
notes by Vernon J. Bourke*
    D28a Book III, Part 1—95¢
    D28b Book III, Part 2—95¢

ON THE TRUTH OF THE
CATHOLIC FAITH
*Summa Contra Gentiles Book
IV: Salvation. Newly translated,
with an Introduction and notes,
By Charles J. O'Neil* D29—95¢

THE WORLD'S FIRST LOVE
By Fulton J. Sheen D30—75¢

THE SIGN OF JONAS
By Thomas Merton D31—95¢

PARENTS, CHILDREN AND THE
FACTS OF LIFE   *By Henry V.
Sattler, C.SS.R.*   D32—75¢

LIGHT ON THE MOUNTAIN : *The
Story of La Salette
By John S. Kennedy* D33—65¢

EDMUND CAMPION
By Evelyn Waugh D34—75¢

HUMBLE POWERS
By Paul Horgan D35—75¢

SAINT THOMAS AQUINAS
By G. K. Chesterton D36—75¢

APOLOGIA PRO VITA SUA
*By John Henry Cardinal New-
man   Introduction by Philip
Hughes*   D37—95¢

A HANDBOOK OF THE CATHOLIC
FAITH
*By Dr. N. G. M. Van Doornik,
Rev. S. Jelsma, Rev. A. Van De
Lisdonk. Ed. Rev. John Green-
wood*   D38—$1.45

THE NEW TESTAMENT
Official Catholic edition
    D39—95¢

MARIA CHAPDELAINE
By Louis Hémon D40—65¢

SAINT AMONG THE HURONS
By Francis X. Talbot, S.J.
    D41—95¢

THE PATH TO ROME
By Hilaire Belloc D42—85¢

SORROW BUILT A BRIDGE
By Katherine Burton D43—85¢

THE WISE MAN FROM THE WEST
By Vincent Cronin D44—85¢

EXISTENCE AND THE EXISTENT
By Jacques Maritain D45—75¢

THE STORY OF THE TRAPP
FAMILY SINGERS
By Maria Augusta Trapp
    D46—95¢

THE WORLD, THE FLESH AND
FATHER SMITH
By Bruce Marshall D47—75¢

THE CHRIST OF CATHOLICISM
By Dom Aelred Graham
    D48—95¢

SAINT FRANCIS XAVIER
By James Brodrick, S.J.
    D49—95¢

SAINT FRANCIS OF ASSISI
By G. K. Chesterton D50—65¢

11

Image Books

...making the world's finest
Catholic literature available to all

VIPERS' TANGLE
by François Mauriac   D51—75¢

THE MANNER IS ORDINARY
by John LaFarge, S.J. D52—95¢

MY LIFE FOR MY SHEEP
by Alfred Duggan   D53—90¢

THE CHURCH AND THE RECON-STRUCTION OF THE MODERN WORLD: *The Social Encyclicals of Pius XI.* Edited by T. P. Mc-Laughlin, C.S.B.   D54—$1.25

A GILSON READER: *Selections from the Writings of Etienne Gilson.* Edited by Anton C. Pegis.
D55—95¢

THE AUTOBIOGRAPHY OF ST. THERESE OF LISIEUX: *The Story of a Soul. A new translation by* John Beevers.   D56—65¢

HELENA
by Evelyn Waugh   D57—65¢

THE GREATEST BIBLE STORIES
A Catholic Anthology from World Literature. Edited by Anne Fremantle.   D58—75¢

THE CITY OF GOD—St. Augustine. Edited with Intro. by Vernon J. Bourke. Foreword by Etienne Gilson.   D59—$1.45

SUPERSTITION CORNER
by Sheila Kaye-Smith D60—65¢

SAINTS AND OURSELVES
Ed. by Philip Caraman, S.J.
D61—95¢

CANA IS FOREVER
by Charles Hugo Doyle
D62—75¢

ASCENT OF MOUNT CARMEL—St. John of the Cross. Translated and Edited by E. Allison Peers.
D63—$1.25

RELIGION AND THE RISE OF WESTERN CULTURE
by Christopher Dawson
D64—85¢

PRINCE OF DARKNESS AND OTHER STORIES
by J. F. Powers   D65—85¢

ST. THOMAS MORE
by E. E. Reynolds   D66—95¢

JESUS AND HIS TIMES
2 Volumes   D67A—95¢
by Daniel-Rops   D67B—95¢

ST. BENEDICT
by Justin McCann, O.S.B.
D68—85¢

THE LITTLE FLOWERS OF ST. FRANCIS
Edited and Translated by
Raphael Brown.   D69—95¢

THE QUIET LIGHT
by Louis de Wohl   D70—95¢

CHARACTERS OF THE REFORMATION
by Hilaire Belloc   D71—85¢

THE BELIEF OF CATHOLICS
by Ronald Knox   D72—75¢

FAITH AND FREEDOM
by Barbara Ward   D73—95¢

GOD AND INTELLIGENCE IN MODERN PHILOSOPHY
by Fulton J. Sheen   D74—95¢

If your bookseller is unable to supply certain titles, write to Image Books, Department MIB, Garden City, New York, stating the titles you desire and enclosing the price of each book (plus 5¢ per book to cover cost of postage and handling). Prices are subject to change without notice.

Image Books

*... making the world's finest
Catholic literature available to all ...*

THE IDEA OF A UNIVERSITY
*by John Henry
Cardinal Newman,
with an Introduction by
George N. Shuster*

One of the most enduring masterpieces of the brilliant nineteenth century scholar.
D75—$1.35

PLAYED BY EAR
by Daniel A. Lord, S.J.

The inspiring and heart-warming autobiography of one of America's most beloved priests.
D76—95¢

MY BELOVED: The Story of a Carmelite Nun
by Mother Catherine Thomas

Revealing, behind-the-scenes view of religious life inside the walls of Carmel. **D77—75¢**

DARK NIGHT OF THE SOUL
*by St. John of the Cross,
edited and translated by
E. Allison Peers*

The magnificent spiritual classic of one of the greatest mystics of all times. **D78—75¢**

TERESA OF AVILA
*by Marcelle Auclair, translated
by Kathleen Pond*

Penetrating portrait of the superb woman renowned as mystic, theologian, author and saint.
D79—$1.35

SAINT PETER THE APOSTLE
by William Thomas Walsh

Exciting biography of the Prince of Apostles who was Keeper of the Keys and first pope.
D80—95¢

THE LOVE OF GOD
by Dom Aelred Graham, O.S.B.

A modern classic on the spiritual life by the distinguished Benedictine scholar. **D81—85¢**

WOMAN OF THE PHARISEES
*by François Mauriac, translated
by Gerard Hopkins*

A dramatic novel—subtle portrait of self-love at its most vindictive, by the world-famous Nobel Prize winner. **D82—75¢**

If your bookseller is unable to supply certain titles, write to Image Books, Department MIB, Garden City, New York, stating the titles you desire and enclosing the price of each book (plus 5¢ per book to cover cost of postage and handling). Prices are subject to change without notice.

Image Books

*. . . making the world's finest
Catholic literature available to all . . .*

THE PILLAR OF FIRE
by Karl Stern
Absorbing story of an eminent psychiatrist's spiritual journey from Judaism to Catholicism.
D83—85¢

ORTHODOXY
by G. K. Chesterton
One of the most enduring masterpieces of 20th-century Catholicism's outstanding literary figure. **D84—75¢**

THIS IS CATHOLICISM
by John J. Walsh, S.J.
Comprehensive and authoritative question-and-answer explanation of the Catholic religion.
D85—$1.25

MEDIEVAL ESSAYS
by Christopher Dawson
Brilliant study of Christian culture, its origins and its influence.
D86—95¢

VESSEL OF CLAY
by Leo Trese
Informal, informative revelations of a parish priest's daily life.
D87—65¢

SAINTS FOR SINNERS
by Alban Goodier, S.J.
Nine saints whose varied roads to sanctity have deep significance for modern men and women.
D88—65¢

THE LONG LONELINESS
by Dorothy Day
Stirring autobiography of an unusual and dedicated woman.
D89—85¢

THIS IS THE MASS
by Henri Daniel-Rops
Introduction by Fulton J. Sheen
Illustrations by Karsh
The Mass eloquently described by Daniel-Rops and graphically illustrated by Karsh photographs of Bishop Sheen. **D90—95¢**

23

Image Books

. . . making the world's finest
Catholic literature available to all . . .

THE ORIGIN OF THE JESUITS
by James Brodrick, S.J.
An absorbing chronicle of the events and characters involved in the founding of one of the Church's greatest orders, the Society of Jesus. **D91–85¢**

A POPULAR HISTORY OF THE REFORMATION
by Philip Hughes
A popular and comprehensive presentation of the characters and events of the Reformation, told by an outstanding Catholic historian. **D92–95¢**

THE RESTLESS FLAME
by Louis de Wohl
An exciting novel of St. Augustine and his times. **D93–85¢**

PROGRESS AND RELIGION
by Christopher Dawson
A thorough analysis of the concept of progress in world history, its development through the centuries, gradual decline, and position today. **D94–85¢**

SCHOLASTICISM AND POLITICS
by Jacques Maritain
Thought-provoking reflections of the world-famed philosopher on the human person—what he is, the basis for his innate dignity, what is true human freedom, and the meaning and ultimate destiny of human life. **D98–95¢**

THE CATHOLIC CHURCH IN THE MODERN WORLD
by E. E. Y. Hales
A panoramic survey of the Catholic Church and her role in world affairs from the French Revolution to the Hungarian uprising in 1956. **D95–95¢**

THE LIFE of Teresa of Jesus
by St. Teresa of Avila
Trans. by E. Allison Peers
One of the great spiritual classics of all times—the autobiography of the renowned mystic and saint—in the definitive English translation. **D96–$1.25**

GIANTS OF THE FAITH
by John A. O'Brien
Revealing portraits of six great figures and their far-reaching effects on the history of Christianity. **D97–95¢**

THE SON OF GOD
by Karl Adam
A brilliant dissertation on the proofs of the divinity of Christ and a searching analysis of the belief that He is true man and true God. **D99–85¢**

THE MAN WHO WAS CHESTERTON
Ed. Raymond T. Bond
A superb collection from the writings of the inimitable G.K. presenting the brilliant literary genius at his scintillating best. **Ð100–$1.45**

If your bookseller is unable to supply certain titles, write to Image Books, Department MIB, Garden City, New York, stating the titles you desire and enclosing the price of each book (plus 5¢ per book to cover cost of postage and handling). Prices are subject to change without notice.

Image Books

THE CONFESSIONS OF ST. AUGUSTINE
Translated, with an introduction and notes, by John K. Ryan

The greatest spiritual autobiography of all times, in a distinguished new translation for the modern reader. **D101—$1.25**

HEART IN PILGRIMAGE
By Evelyn Eaton and Edward Roberts Moore

A moving novel based on the life of Mother Seton, foundress of the Sisters of Charity.
D102—75¢

ESSAY ON THE DEVELOPMENT OF CHRISTIAN DOCTRINE
By John Henry Cardinal Newman. Introduction by Gustave Weigel, S.J.

The celebrated study of the development of Catholic doctrine through the ages, by the greatest religious thinker of modern times. **D105—$1.35**

BABY GROWS IN AGE AND GRACE
By Sister Mary de Lourdes

An invaluable practical guide for the physical, mental and spiritual training of the preschool child. **D104—75¢**

THE STORY OF AMERICAN CATHOLICISM, 2 Volumes
By Theodore Maynard

An authoritative and concise history of the Catholic Church in America and its contribution to American political and social development. **D106A—95¢**
D106B—95¢

THE HEART OF MAN
By Gerald Vann, O.P.

Unique and compassionate insights into man — his nature, problems, aspirations and relation to God. **D103—75¢**

THE CASE OF CORNELIA CONNELLY
By Juliana Wadham

More dramatic than fiction is this inspiring biography of Cornelia Connelly, wife, mother, nun, and possibly saint.
D107—85¢

UNDERSTANDING EUROPE
By Christopher Dawson

A penetrating analysis of the historical forces and backgrounds that led to present world tensions, by the outstanding historian of Western Culture.
D108—85¢

✠ IMAGE BOOKS

Image Books constitute a quality library of Catholic writings, broad in human interest and deep in Christian insight. They will include classical Christian writings, devotion, philosophy, education and history; biographies, novels and poetry; and books on contemporary social problems. They represent a planned program of making available to the widest possible audience the finest Catholic literature in attractive, paper-bound, inexpensive editions. They have been selected with these criteria in mind: that they must in every instance be well written, inspiring to the spirit, and of lasting value to the general audience who will purchase them.

The majority of Image Books will consist of reprints made possible through the cooperation of the publishers of the original editions. Occasionally certain much-needed volumes which are not available will also be initiated for this series.

A descriptive catalogue of the Image Books already published may be obtained by writing directly to the publisher. Comments and suggestions from those interested in the series are welcomed by the publisher.　　　　　　　　　　　　　3